CW00500917

THE RUTH PRETTY COOKBOOK

PENGUIN BOOKS

PENGUIN BOOKS

Penguin Books (NZ) Ltd, cnr Airborne and Rosedale Roads, Albany,
Auckland 1310, New Zealand
Penguin Books Ltd, 80 Strand, London, WC2R 0RL, England
Penguin Putnam Inc, 375 Hudson Street, New York, NY 10014, United States
Penguin Books Australia Ltd, 250 Camberwell Road, Camberwell,
Victoria 3124, Australia
Penguin Books Canada Ltd, 10 Alcorn Avenue, Toronto,
Ontario, Canada M4V 3B2
Penguin Books (South Africa) (Pty) Ltd, 24 Sturdee Avenue, Rosebank,
Johannesburg 2196, South Africa,
Penguin Books India (P) Ltd, 11, Community Centre, Panchsheel Park,
New Delhi 110 017, India
Penguin Books Ltd, Registered Offices: Harmondsworth, Middlesex, England

First published by Penguin Books (NZ) Ltd, 2002

1 3 5 7 9 10 8 6 4 2

Copyright © text and photographs Ruth Pretty, 2002

The right of Ruth Pretty to be identified as the author of this work in terms of section 96 of the
Copyright Act 1994 is hereby asserted.

Designed and typeset by Seven
Printed by Bookbuilders, Hong Kong

All rights reserved. Without limiting the rights under copyright reserved above,
no part of this publication may be reproduced, stored in or introduced
into a retrieval system, or transmitted, in any form or by any means
(electronic, mechanical, photocopying, recording or otherwise), without
the prior written permission of both the copyright owner and
the above publisher of this book.

ISBN 0 14 301842 6
www.penguin.co.nz

THE
RUTH PRETTY
COOKBOOK

Photography by Murray Lloyd

PENGUIN BOOKS

CONTENTS

INTRODUCTION

I can hardly wait to get out of bed in the morning and go to work as I love to cook and my job is all about cooking. I never planned my career, and had no idea when I began cooking twenty-five years ago that it would encompass so many aspects of cooking: teaching, writing, speaking, as well as actually cooking.

I can sense a cook a mile away; they are always warm, embracing people. I have never met a person who enjoys cooking that I have not instantly liked.

I have the immense pleasure of spending every day with people who love to cook. The chefs in our kitchen are happiest when their daily prep list is finished, and they have the opportunity to make a dish they have never tried before; or when they see a batch of shimmering jam lined up or a wedding cake departing to its reception. But their greatest satisfaction is when all the hard work comes together at the planned event, and they are able to see the faces of delighted guests.

All good chefs work hard; they are creators, organisers and pragmatists. A good chef always walks quickly and knows how to follow through.

I am fortunate to come into daily contact with people I don't know and may never meet but who love to cook. They are the readers who respond to my weekly column in the *Dominion Post*. People email or ring to tell me if a recipe has exceeded their expectations, to let me know if I have made a mistake, or to tell me more about the recipes. Sometimes they even share their favourite recipe with me. And I love it!

The youngest cooking school student at our school was fourteen, and the oldest ninety-one. These students have diverse occupations, but all share a love of cooking. I enjoy hearing about their childhood food experiences, what they cook for their families and how they spend celebratory days.

They also tell me about cooking episodes that went really wrong for them, but more often how they exceeded the expectations of their family and friends with their culinary delights.

Then there are our catering clients whose ideas have inspired many of the recipes in this book. Their feedback has helped to evolve my style of cooking and give me the confidence to believe that when it comes to food, less is always more.

A cook would be nothing without good products, and my suppliers delight me daily with their fresh and innovative produce. They reinforce my belief that passion and tenacity are worth more in a working life than monetary rewards. I share in the pride they have in their produce when clients tell me that I am serving the tastiest tomatoes or the most luscious strawberries they have ever eaten.

This book is dedicated to my mother, who always encouraged my creativity and instilled in me a joy of cooking. And to my father, who made me believe that service is a customer's right and that to serve is indeed noble. It is also dedicated to every person who loves to cook and is prepared to share this gift with others, and to every chef I have ever worked with who has given me tiny or big pieces to add to my ever-growing jigsaw of food knowledge.

The Ruth Pretty Cookbook contains the recipes I like to cook for catering clients, or share with cooking class students and cook at home for my own family and friends.

Thank you to Murray Lloyd who photographed my food so it looked like my food, and to Kirsten Jolly who styled the food so fabulously. Thank you to Jo-Anne Tracey, who tested and retested many of the recipes, and to Nicolette Gregory for her patience in putting together my manuscript. Thank you to my husband, Paul, who has always loved my cooking and encouraged my career every step of the way.

BRUNCH

Celebrate your next birthday with a brunch party.
This is the meal I relish more than any other meal,
but which I indulge in the most infrequently.

It is a perfect way to entertain because it can be
spontaneous and, depending on your intake of
champagne, allows you and your guests the rest
of the day to do other things. Remember that good
coffee is as important at brunch as champagne.

ESPRESSO SCRAMBLED EGGS

If you have an espresso machine at home try this unusual method. Chef Graham Brown told me that when he owned a restaurant, he made eggs this way as a late-night snack for his staff. These scrambled eggs are light and fluffy and produce greater volume than other methods. Very handy on a gourmet camping trip.

←

Espresso Scrambled Eggs

1 LARGE SERVING

2 eggs
2 tblsp cream
Maldon sea salt and freshly ground black pepper
1 tblsp chopped parsley or chopped tarragon or chives
3 tsp butter (optional)

- Combine eggs and cream in the stainless-steel jug you use to froth milk and beat with a fork.
- Add salt and pepper and herbs and stir to combine. If using butter, dice it very small and add now.
- Give the steam jet a blast to ensure that any steam which has condensated is removed from the jet.
- Place jug under the steam jet, with the steam jet tip just below the egg mixture surface. Turn the steam jet on full.
- Swirl the jug, keeping steam jet tip in the egg mixture and continue this movement until egg is cooked.
- Transfer contents of jug onto a plate and accompany with a slice of hot buttered toast and a strong Bloody Mary.

Note: After you have made your scrambled eggs, it is critical to give the steam jet a blast to remove any egg which may be left in the jet arm. Wash the jet arm well.

MELON AND CRISPY PROSCIUTTO WITH MANUKA HONEY AND MUSTARD DRESSING

A very refreshing brunch dish, particularly good with a glass of riesling.

→

Melon and Crispy
Prosciutto with
Manuka Honey and
Mustard Dressing

SERVES 6–8

60g thinly sliced prosciutto (cut in half lengthways)
1 rock melon (cut into 6–8 wedges lengthways)
1 recipe Manuka Honey and Mustard Dressing (below)

+ Preheat oven to 150°C.
+ Lie prosciutto strips between 2 sheets of baking paper and bake for 5–7 minutes or until lightly browned and crispy. Allow to cool.
+ Separate skin from melon and arrange melon in skin on platter.
+ Stand crispy prosciutto upright against melon and drizzle melon with Manuka Honey and Mustard Dressing.

MANUKA HONEY AND MUSTARD DRESSING

MAKES 200ML

85ml (⅓ cup) white vinegar
15g (1 tblsp) sugar
3g (1 clove) garlic (peeled and crushed)
15g (1 tblsp) wholegrain mustard
15ml (1 tblsp) manuka honey
Maldon sea salt and freshly ground black pepper
100ml olive oil

+ Place all ingredients (except olive oil) in a food processor and, with the food processor running, slowly pour in the olive oil (dressing will thicken slightly).
+ Taste for seasoning and pour into a sterilised jar. Cover and refrigerate until required.

QUICK WHOLEMEAL BREAD

This is so quick it can happen while you are having a shower. Add raisins or dried figs if you wish, and serve with mascarpone and runny honey. You do not have to use this blend of flours. You can use all white flour or experiment with other flours such as rye or whole wheat.

←
Quick Wholemeal
Bread

MAKES 1 24 X 13CM LOAF

2 tsp honey
250ml (1 cup) boiling water
190ml (¾ cup) cold water
14g (3½ tsp) active dried yeast granules
220g wholemeal flour
230g (1⅔ cups) flour (preferably
    bakers')
2 tsp Maldon sea salt
20g pumpkin seeds (optional)

+ Preheat oven to 80°C to prove dough.
+ In a large bowl, combine honey and boiling water. Stir until honey is dissolved.
+ Add cold water to honey mixture and stir to combine.
+ Sprinkle yeast over honey mixture and cover bowl with plastic wrap. Place bowl in a warm area until mixture is bubbly and slightly risen, approximately 15 minutes. This mixture is the 'sponge'.
+ In a separate bowl combine flours and salt. Set aside.
+ Once the 'sponge' mixture is ready, whisk vigorously until frothy.
+ Gradually incorporate flour mixture into 'sponge' mixture, beating with a wooden spoon.
+ Spray a 24 x 13cm non-stick loaf tin and pour dough into tin (the dough will be very wet). Sprinkle dough with pumpkin seeds.
+ Allow dough to prove in the preheated oven for 20 minutes or until dough is level with top of tin. It may rise above top of tin during this time, so do not be concerned!
+ Without removing bread from oven, raise oven temperature to 210°C, and bake for a further 30 minutes or until loaf sounds hollow when tapped. Turn bread out onto a cooling rack and allow to cool.

SWISS MUESLI

A good coffee and a bowl of Swiss Muesli is a very bright start to the day. Don't necessarily
stick to this recipe – add whatever fruit or nuts take your fancy.

→
Swiss Muesli

SERVES 6–8

200g (2 cups) rolled oats
310ml (1¼ cups) cold water
5g (2 tblsp) bran
100g (¾ cup) toasted nuts (mix of
   hazelnuts, almonds or pistachios)
300g (2 small) Granny Smith apples
   (peeled and grated)
360g (2 small) bananas (diced)
125ml (½ cup) natural yoghurt
40ml (3 tblsp) liquid honey
150g (¾ cup) dried apricots (quartered)
fresh fruit for garnish
extra liquid honey (optional)

+ Place the rolled oats and water into a medium
   bowl and soak at room temperature overnight.
+ The following day combine oats with the
   bran, nuts, apple, banana, yoghurt, honey
   and apricots.
+ Garnish with fresh fruit and drizzle with
   liquid honey if you wish. In summer berries
   are great; in winter try passionfruit, bananas
   or feijoas.

Scrambled Eggs and
Baked Sweet and
Sour Tomatoes

SCRAMBLED EGGS

Scrambled eggs with Vogel's toast is my all-time favourite comfort food. If you dare, increase the cream in this recipe. Organic free-range eggs move scrambled eggs to another dimension.

1 LARGE SERVING

2 eggs
2 tblsp cream
Maldon sea salt and freshly ground
  black pepper
1 tblsp chopped parsley or chopped
  tarragon or chives
3 tsp butter

+ Combine eggs and cream in a small bowl and beat with a fork.
+ Add salt and pepper and herbs and stir to combine.
+ Melt 1 tsp butter in a small heavy–based pot. Pour in egg mixture. Cook over a low heat and with a wooden spoon lift and turn the mixture. In the last minutes of cooking, add remaining butter and gently fold through.
+ Transfer contents of pot onto a plate and accompany with Vogel's toast.

BAKED SWEET AND SOUR TOMATOES

Perfect to serve with scrambled eggs and bacon. This method really intensifies the tomato flavour. If you are into kitchen gadgets like I am, use a tomato corer.

SERVES 4

400–500g (4 large) round tomatoes
10g (2 tsp) butter (softened)
30g (2½ tblsp) brown sugar
1 clove garlic (peeled and crushed)

+ Preheat oven to 100°C.
+ Cut a 1.5–2cm cavity in the top of each tomato, removing the core at the same time.
+ Mix butter, brown sugar and garlic to a paste. Push butter mixture into tomato cavity.
+ Place tomatoes on a baking tray and bake for one hour.
+ Serve hot or warm.

CRAYFISH OMELETTE

This is the ultimate easy-to-make and delightful-to-eat brunch dish. Serve with a glass of Veuve Clicquot and forget about Monday's problems. You can split the cooked crayfish in half lengthways to give you two serves from one crayfish tail. Serve with Lemon Potato Wedges with Oregano (see page 21).

→

Crayfish Omelette

SERVES 1

1 (400–600g) small live crayfish
15g (1 tblsp) butter
1 clove garlic (peeled and chopped)
1 small shallot (peeled and chopped)
Maldon sea salt and freshly ground
　　black pepper
2 eggs
30ml (2 tblsp) cream
30g (2 tblsp) butter

+ Drown crayfish in cold water and then plunge it into a pot of boiling, lightly salted water.
+ Cook for 8 minutes (we allow 12 minutes per kg weight) or until crayfish has turned a deep red colour.
+ When crayfish is cool enough to handle remove tail and take the flesh out; keep as a whole piece. Remove intestinal tract and reserve body for another use.
+ Place a small frypan onto medium heat and melt first measure of butter. Add crayfish tail, garlic and shallot. Toss until garlic and shallot has softened, but not browned, and crayfish tail is warmed through and coated with butter. Season with salt and pepper.
+ Lightly whisk eggs, cream and seasoning to taste.
+ Place another small frypan onto heat and melt second measure of butter.
+ Pour egg mixture into frypan and slowly cook until base is golden brown but centre of omelette is still moist.
+ Place crayfish tail on one side of omelette and flip the other side over it.
+ Serve immediately drizzled with buttery juices from crayfish frypan.

LEMON POTATO WEDGES WITH OREGANO

For this dish I like to use either Desirèe or Agria potatoes.

←

**Lemon Potato
Wedges with
Oregano**

SERVES 8

**1.6kg large potatoes (peeled)
250ml (1 cup) water
125ml (½ cup) lemon juice
125ml (½ cup) olive oil
3 tblsp freshly chopped Greek
  oregano
1 tblsp Maldon sea salt
¼ tsp freshly ground
  black pepper**

Preheat oven to 220ºC.

Cut potatoes into 4–6 wedges (depending on the size of the potato). Aim for large wedges. Place potatoes in a non-reactive roasting tray and combine with remaining ingredients. Toss potatoes until well coated.

Bake potatoes, uncovered, for 30 minutes, then using a scraper, turn potatoes over so they brown evenly. Add a little more water if the liquid has evaporated.

Reduce oven temperature to 180ºC and bake potatoes for a further 45–60 minutes, or until fork-tender and brown on the edges.

LITTLE POPOVERS WITH SOUR CREAM AND SALMON CAVIAR

These are called Popovers because they do pop over the tin. If you are entertaining a crowd
at brunch, this is an excellent dish to pass around while guests are mingling before the main event.

→
**Little Popovers with
Sour Cream and
Salmon Caviar**

MAKES 12

1 egg (lightly whisked)
70g (½ cup) flour (sifted)
¼ tsp salt
125ml (½ cup) milk
15g (1 tblsp) melted butter
125g sour cream
1 jar Salmon Caviar

+ Prepare baby muffin tins with baking spray.
+ Place egg, flour, salt, milk and melted butter
  in a bowl and mix with a wooden spoon.
+ Pour mixture into prepared baby muffin tins,
  filling muffin tins to only two-thirds full.
+ Place popovers in a cold oven.
+ Set oven to 200ºC and bake for 15–20
  minutes until golden brown.
+ Place tray on a cooling rack, remove
  popovers from tins and top warmed
  popovers with a heaped teaspoon of sour
  cream and a dollop of Salmon Caviar.

←

**Chocolate Mud
Pastries**

CHOCOLATE MUD PASTRIES

I am giving you a recipe for twenty-four because I recommend you freeze one tray (uncooked) for your next brunch party. Bake straight from freezer at the temperature in the recipe.

MAKES 24

250g puff pastry
150g dark chocolate
60g (6 tblsp) unsalted butter
155g (¾ cup plus 4½ tblsp)
  castor sugar
2 eggs
1 tsp pure vanilla essence
14g (2 tblsp) flour (sifted)

- Prepare muffin tins with baking spray.
- Roll out pastry on a floured bench into a 27cm square. Cut pastry into 24 7.5cm squares.
- Press each pastry square into the bottom of a prepared muffin cup.
- Preheat oven to 200°C.
- Rest pastry for 20–30 minutes in the refrigerator.
- Meanwhile, put chocolate and butter into a pot set over another pot of simmering water. Gently melt chocolate and butter and then stir in sugar. The chocolate mixture should only be warm.
- Whisk eggs and vanilla together and add to chocolate mixture. Stir in flour.
- Spoon 1 tblsp chocolate mixture into the centre of each pastry cup.
- Bake for 15–20 minutes or until pastry is golden. Remove mud pastries from muffin pans onto a cooling rack.
- Dust with icing sugar to serve.

CARAMELISED PEAR BREAKFAST CAKES

These breakfast cakes can be prepared in advance and frozen uncooked. Cook directly from freezer, allowing a little extra cooking time. Serve with thick Greek-style yoghurt.

→
**Caramelised Pear
Breakfast Cakes**

MAKES 12 BREAKFAST CAKES

3–4 medium pears (peeled and cored)
70g (7 tblsp) butter
100g (½ cup) brown sugar
**185g (1⅓ cups) flour (preferably
   high grade)**
135g (⅔ cup) sugar
1½ tsp cinnamon
1 tsp baking soda
½ tsp ground ginger
½ tsp salt
**45g (3 tblsp) crystallised ginger
   (finely chopped)**
3 eggs
125ml (½ cup) canola oil
5ml (1 tsp) vanilla essence
1½ tsp grated orange zest

+ Preheat oven to 180°C.
+ Prepare pears. Cut 2 pears through the waist. Cut 1cm slices lengthways through the 'bottom' halves. Grate the remaining 'top' halves and make up to 1 cup (150g) by grating remaining pears.
+ For the caramelised pears, melt butter and pour evenly into 12 sprayed muffin tins. Sprinkle brown sugar (about 2 heaped tsp) and arrange 2 pear slices in base of each tin. Place the tins in refrigerator to set the butter while you prepare breakfast cake mixture.
+ In a bowl sieve together flour, sugar, cinnamon, baking soda, ground ginger and salt. Add finely chopped crystallised ginger.
+ In a second bowl whisk together eggs, oil, vanilla and orange zest. Add grated pears and mix until just combined.
+ Mix dry ingredients with wet ingredients until just combined. Do not overmix or the breakfast cakes will be tough. Carefully pour batter over pears to fill muffin tins.
+ Bake for 15–20 minutes or until a skewer inserted comes out clean. Allow to stand in tin for 5 minutes before removing.
+ Serve upside down.

BLACKCURRANT AND WHITE CHOCOLATE BRIOCHE

Rich buttery yeast cakes oozing with sweet and sour syrupy fruit. We always use frozen blackcurrants because they come already destalked.

MAKES 8 LITTLE CAKES

35g (3 tblsp) butter (melted) for
  greasing moulds
40g (4 tblsp) sugar for sprinkling into
  moulds (plus extra to sweeten
  blackcurrants if desired)
210g (1½ cups) destalked blackcurrants
80g (½ cup) white chocolate buttons
1 recipe Best-ever Brioche Dough (below)
1 egg (lightly beaten)
icing sugar for dusting

+ Liberally butter 8 9cm diameter brioche moulds or muffin tins and sprinkle with sugar.
+ If desired, toss blackcurrants in a little sugar to sweeten.
+ Punch cold dough down and divide into 9 pieces (reserve one piece of dough for jaunty topknots on brioche). Divide blackcurrants and white chocolate buttons into 8 piles.
+ Roll out each piece of dough into a round (approximately 16cm in diameter). Place a pile of blackcurrants and white chocolate buttons in middle of each dough round and pleat dough around fruit to secure it.
+ Put one brioche into each mould. Brush with beaten egg, being careful not to spill too much on the inside of the tin, as this will make it difficult to remove the brioche.
+ To make the topknots: using reserved dough, roll little balls (approximately 1cm in diameter) and place on top (in centre) of brioche. Leave brioche in a warm place for approximately 20–30 minutes, or until the dough does not spring back when pushed.
+ Preheat oven to 200°C. A few minutes before placing brioche in oven, place a shallow baking pan with 2cm boiling water on the floor of the oven or on the lowest shelf.
+ Brush brioche once again with beaten egg and bake for 15–18 minutes or until golden brown.
+ Dust with icing sugar and serve with whipped cream if you wish.

BEST-EVER BRIOCHE DOUGH

MAKES ENOUGH FOR 8 9CM BRIOCHE

60ml (¼ cup) lukewarm water
½ tsp sugar
1 tsp active dried yeast granules
15g (1 tblsp) sugar
225g (1½ cups plus 2 tblsp) flour
  (preferably bakers')
150g butter (roughly diced and softened)
2 egg yolks
1 egg white
½ tsp salt
water as needed
baking spray for greasing bowl

+ In a small bowl combine water, first measure of sugar and yeast. Let stand for 2 minutes until foamy.
+ In the bowl of an electric mixer put second measure of sugar, flour and butter. Mix with paddle attachment until flour and butter are completely blended. Add egg yolks and mix for 30 seconds.
+ Add egg white, salt and yeast mixture and beat to just combine. Dough should not form a ball, but should be a wet and sticky batter. Add a little water if necessary.
+ Transfer dough to a lightly greased bowl, cover with plastic wrap and let dough rise at room temperature for 30–45 minutes (the dough will have risen very little during this time). Refrigerate dough for 45 minutes or overnight if desired. Dough must be cold before it can be punched down and shaped. If it is at room temperature, the butter will ooze out from the dough.
+ Use dough as required.

TOFFEE STRAWBERRIES

A simple ending to a brunch meal. Sometimes you only need a tiny piece of something sweet. Dip the strawberries on the day you require them and store at room temperature. Do not refrigerate.

→

**Toffee
Strawberries**
Top dish

→

**The Ultimate
Chocolate-dipped
Long-stemmed
Strawberries**
Bottom dish

YIELDS 30

200g (1 cup) sugar
125ml (½ cup) water
**1kg (or about 30) long-stemmed
strawberries**

+ In a small pot place sugar and water. Over a medium heat, using a metal spoon, stir until sugar is dissolved.
+ Increase heat and bring sugar solution to the boil. Boil (do not stir sugar solution while it is boiling) until the syrup is a golden brown colour. It may take 10–12 minutes.
+ If sugar crystals form on the side of the pot, use a clean pastry brush dipped in cold water to occasionally brush sugar crystals down into the boiling sugar solution.
+ When syrup has reached golden brown colour, remove pot from heat.
+ Tip pot on an angle and, holding strawberry by the stem, dip half to three-quarters of strawberry in toffee.
+ Place dipped strawberries on a tray lined with aluminium foil and leave to set (this will only take a few minutes).
+ Using a flexible metal spatula, remove strawberries from tray and eat within a few hours.

THE ULTIMATE CHOCOLATE-DIPPED LONG-STEMMED STRAWBERRIES

Strawberries for dipping must be picked in dry weather, held at room temperature and dipped when very fresh. If strawberries are at all damp from the weather or the fridge, liquid will seep through the chocolate. Dip strawberries on the day you require them. Store them in a covered plastic container with wax paper between each layer.

YIELDS 30

360g dark chocolate (buttons or pieces, good quality Belgian or French)
**1kg (or about 30) long-stemmed
strawberries**

+ Melt the chocolate in a double boiler: a double boiler can be as simple as a bowl set over a pot, but the bowl needs to fit the pot snugly. Pour warm water into pot but not so much that it touches the base of the bowl. Place the chocolate in the bowl and heat the water in pot to simmering only. Do not allow the water to get hot – heat affects chocolate adversely. Boiling water produces steam that will fall back into the chocolate, steam equals water and chocolate hates water. As soon as some chocolate begins to melt, remove bowl from heat and stir until the melted chocolate combines with the unmelted chocolate.
+ Holding the strawberry by its stem, dip half to three-quarters in chocolate and place on a baking tray lined with aluminium foil.
+ Place tray in freezer for 4–5 minutes or until chocolate is firm. With a flexible metal spatula remove strawberries from tray. Store at room temperature until required.

NEW ZEALAND IN CUBES

A very refreshing and colourful punch. Children love this drink. Make in long, tall glasses and serve immediately.

**New Zealand
in Cubes**

SERVES 6

450ml Schweppes lemonade
450ml Lemon and Paeroa
1 recipe Juice Cubes (below)

+ Place a cube of each variety into each highball glass, stacking cubes as best you can.
+ Pour equal quantities of Schweppes lemonade and Lemon and Paeroa into glasses.
+ Drink slowly, relishing the melting flavours.

JUICE CUBES

3 kiwifruit, peeled
**150ml Ocean Spray Ruby Red
  Grapefruit Juice**
150ml Ocean Spray Cranberry Juice
150ml freshly squeezed orange juice
150ml Lemon and Paeroa

+ Place kiwifruit in a food processor with plastic blade and process until fruit is pulpy.
+ Pour into a sieve placed over a bowl and push pulp through the sieve. Retain the pulp and discard the seeds.
+ Place kiwifruit pulp into 6–8 ice cube moulds and freeze.
+ Pour the fruit juices and Lemon and Paeroa into ice cube trays, making 6–8 cubes of each variety.
+ Place the trays in the freezer for at least 4 hours or until frozen. If not using immediately, store in plastic bags.

→

**Herb Crumbed
Scallops with
Tartare Sauce**

recipe page 36

PASSAROUNDS

Because cocktail parties are an important part of a caterer's life, passarounds are high on our kitchen's creativity list. Passarounds should be one or two bite-sized explosions of flavour. At home, do not attempt detailed, fiddly passarounds! Serve big, bold platters of more simple food.

HERB CRUMBED SCALLOPS WITH TARTARE SAUCE

Scallops can be crumbed one day ahead if dried well before crumbing and stored in a covered container in the fridge. We make fresh breadcrumbs by crumbing leftover bread in the food processor, then freeze the breadcrumbs until we need them (see picture page 35).

MAKES 30 PASSAROUNDS

30 scallops
2 cups fresh breadcrumbs
½ cup chopped herbs (a mix of Italian
    parsley, chervil and parsley)
Maldon sea salt and freshly ground
    black pepper
¼ cup flour
2 eggs (lightly beaten)
clarified butter for cooking
lemon juice
Tartare Sauce (opposite)

+ Wash scallops and remove any grit and the intestinal tract, but be careful not to remove the roe from the scallops during cleaning. Pat scallops dry with paper towels.
+ Combine breadcrumbs with herbs and seasoning.
+ Line a tray with plastic wrap. Pass scallops through flour, eggs and breadcrumbs and place onto the tray (if you need to, place plastic wrap between each layer). Leave for at least 1–2 hours to allow the crumbs to adhere.
+ Heat a heavy-based frypan (or barbecue flat plate) and add clarified butter so you have a generous layer on the cooking surface. Shallow fry scallops for 2–3 minutes on each side or until golden brown.
+ Drain scallops on paper towels. Sprinkle with lemon juice and season with salt and pepper.
+ Serve with Tartare Sauce.

TARTARE SAUCE

Store covered in the fridge for up to five days.

MAKES 1½ CUPS

30g (2 tblsp) finely chopped capers
3 spring onions (chopped)
75g (½ cup) finely chopped gherkins
1 cup Quick Food Processor
   Mayonnaise (below)
¼ cup finely chopped Italian parsley
1 tblsp lemon juice
¼ cup finely chopped chervil
Maldon sea salt and freshly ground
   black pepper

+   Combine all ingredients.

QUICK FOOD PROCESSOR MAYONNAISE

I love olive oil, but sometimes salad oil is useful in mayonnaise because of its non-descriptive taste.

MAKES 1¼ CUPS

2 egg yolks
½ tblsp lemon juice
Maldon sea salt and freshly ground
   black pepper
250ml (1 cup) salad oil

+   Place egg yolks, lemon juice, salt and freshly ground black pepper and ¼ cup of salad oil in a food processor fitted with a metal blade. Blend for 10 seconds.
+   With the food processor going, pour the remaining salad oil very slowly through the feeder tube until all of the oil is combined. Store in the refrigerator.

BARBECUED BABY PIZZAS

Children love to help cook these pizzas. Use bakers' flour or strong flour for the dough, and if rye flour is hard to buy, increase the quantity of bakers' flour.

MAKES 25–30 BABY PIZZAS

1½ tsp powdered yeast
125ml (½ cup) warm water
½ tsp sugar
1½ tsp salt
14g (2 tblsp) rye flour
210g (1½ cups) bakers' flour
75ml (¼ cup and 1 tblsp) olive oil
extra olive oil for oiling rising bowl

Topping:
300g pesto
120g bocconcini (sliced into thin rounds)
30g Parmesan cheese (grated or finely shaved)

+ Combine yeast, water and sugar in a small bowl.
+ Cover bowl with plastic wrap and leave in a warm place until mixture starts to foam.
+ Put salt, rye flour and flour into a food processor fitted with a metal blade.
+ Add olive oil to the yeast mixture.
+ With the food processor running, pour yeast and olive oil mixture through the feed tube.
+ Process until the mixture forms a ball. You may need to add a little more water.
+ Oil a china or glass bowl and transfer the ball of dough to the bowl. Cover bowl with plastic wrap and leave in a warm place until dough has doubled in size.
+ Punch dough down, knead and return to the oiled bowl.
+ Cover bowl with plastic wrap and leave dough to rise again until it has doubled in size.
+ Heat a barbecue or, if you prefer, a heavy cast-iron frypan.
+ Break off little balls of dough (each ball 10–15g), and flatten each ball between your hands into a very thin disc.
+ Place dough discs on a baking tray or pizza peel.
+ Slide each dough disc onto barbecue and cook on one side.
+ When the underside is browned, using a spatula, slide pizzas back onto the baking tray or pizza peel, cooked side up.
+ Add topping to the cooked side.
+ Slide the topped pizzas back onto the barbecue and cook until the pizzas are lightly browned.
+ Serve immediately.

TINY TOASTED PESTO SANDWICHES

My friend, Clare Ferguson, cookbook author, suggested this recipe to me. They will be quickly gobbled up by your guests (see picture page 38).

MAKES 32 PASSAROUNDS

1 recipe Sandwich Pesto (below)
16 slices white sandwich bread
Maldon sea salt
190ml (¾ cup) olive oil for cooking
64 small basil leaves

+ Spread a generous layer (about 3 tblsp per slice) of Sandwich Pesto onto half of bread slices. Sprinkle with salt and top with second slice of bread.
+ Using an electric knife remove crusts from sandwiches and then cut each sandwich into 8 small triangles.
+ Heat a heavy-based frypan (or a barbecue flat plate) and add a little oil. Fry sandwiches over moderate heat until golden brown on each side. Drain on absorbent paper. Repeat process until all sandwiches are cooked.

To serve:
+ Thread one basil leaf on a skewer followed by a sandwich, then repeat, resulting in each skewer having 2 basil leaves and 2 sandwiches. Repeat until all sandwiches are on skewers. Serve warm.

SANDWICH PESTO

The small quantity of oil in this recipe means the pesto will not ooze out of the sandwiches.

2 cloves garlic (peeled)
75g (½ cup) pinenuts
90g (1½ cups packed) basil leaves
150g (1 cup) grated Parmesan cheese
85ml (⅓ cup) olive oil
Maldon sea salt and freshly ground
  black pepper
15ml (1 tblsp) lemon juice

+ Place garlic, pinenuts, basil and Parmesan into a food processor fitted with metal blade.
+ With the food processor going, slowly pour in olive oil through the feed tube.
+ Season with salt and pepper and add lemon juice to taste.

MUSSEL AND DILL FRITTERS

If you are cooking the mussels yourself, you need 2kg of mussels in shells to obtain 300g of cooked mussel meat. To cook mussels, place in a pot with ¼ cup of water and a pinch of salt, cover with the lid and steam (see picture page 38).

MAKES 35 PASSAROUNDS

300g cooked mussel meat (minced
   or very finely chopped)
1 egg (lightly beaten)
60g (⅓ cup plus 2 tblsp) flour
45g (½ cup) fresh breadcrumbs
1 tsp Worcestershire sauce
1 (125g) onion (finely chopped)
1 tblsp finely chopped parsley
4 tblsp finely chopped dill
Maldon sea salt and freshly ground
   black pepper
clarified butter for cooking
1 lemon

+ Combine mussel meat, egg, flour, breadcrumbs, Worcestershire sauce, onion, herbs and seasoning in a medium-sized bowl and mix.
+ Heat a heavy-based frypan (or barbecue flat plate) and add enough clarified butter so that when it melts it covers the base of the pan (or flat plate).
+ Drop teaspoonfuls of fritter mix into pan and cook until brown on one side. Turn and cook until brown on the other side.
+ Drain on paper towels and season with lemon juice and salt and pepper.

FIG AND PROSCIUTTO SANDWICHES

A lovely little autumn bite (see picture page 38).

MAKES 32 PASSAROUNDS

8 slices Vogel's sandwich bread
240g (1 cup) cream cheese
approximately 60g (8 thin slices)
   prosciutto (trimmed of fat and torn
   into quarters)
8 ripe figs (stems removed)
mint leaves

+ Remove crusts from bread. Cut each slice into 4 squares and spread cream cheese on one side of each square. Place a folded prosciutto slice on each square.
+ With fig upright, thinly cut 2 opposite sides off. Cut remainder into 4 even slices (more or less, depending on size of fig) and place each slice on prosciutto. Top with a mint leaf.

OLD-FASHIONED SALMON CAKES

We like to serve these with Tartare Sauce (see page 37) or Minted Pea Dip (see page 79).

SERVES 8

15g (1 tblsp) butter
1 tblsp finely chopped shallot
1 recipe Mashed Potato (below)
300g flaked salmon (hot-smoked
    or fresh cooked)
1 egg (lightly beaten)
¼ cup finely chopped spring onions
½ cup finely chopped parsley
juice of 1 lemon
dash of tabasco sauce
Maldon sea salt and freshly ground
    black pepper
2 eggs
30ml (2 tblsp) milk
½ cup finely grated Parmesan cheese
1 cup fresh breadcrumbs
70g (½ cup) flour
clarified butter

+ In a heavy-based frypan melt butter. Once
   hot, add shallots and cook until soft and
   transparent but not browned.
+ Mix together shallot, Mashed Potato, salmon,
   beaten egg, spring onions and parsley.
   Season mixture with lemon juice and
   tabasco. Add salt and pepper to taste.
+ Form mixture into little balls approximately
   2cm in diameter and refrigerate until firm.
+ Lightly beat eggs with milk and season
   with salt and pepper. Combine Parmesan
   and breadcrumbs.
+ Dip each ball in flour, followed by the egg
   mixture, and then roll ball in the Parmesan
   crumbs.
+ In a heated, heavy frypan (or barbecue flat
   plate) melt some clarified butter and cook
   salmon cakes on both sides until they are
   a light golden colour. Drain on paper towels
   and season with lemon juice and salt and
   pepper before serving.

MASHED POTATO

SERVES 8

300g potatoes (peeled and cut into
    even-sized pieces)
15g (1 tblsp) butter
45ml (3 tblsp) cream
Maldon sea salt and freshly ground
    black pepper
pinch ground nutmeg

+ Steam potatoes until soft.
+ Mash potatoes with butter and cream until
   smooth. Season with salt and pepper and
   nutmeg. Once cold, refrigerate until required.

THE WIDOW'S PUFFS

We named these puffs in honour of the Widow Clicquot, the founder of the Champagne house, because they taste so good with her champagne. To save time, cut out pastry circles up to three days in advance, wrap tightly and refrigerate until required. Alternatively, prepare pastry circles up to one month in advance and freeze raw, then cook from frozen, allowing a little extra time for cooking (see picture page 38).

MAKES 30 PASSAROUNDS

flour for dusting bench
240g pre-rolled puff pastry
1 egg yolk
1 tsp cold water
½ tsp salt
4 tsp poppyseeds
1 recipe Sun-dried Tomato
   Pesto (below)

+ Dust bench with flour. Using a 5cm round cutter, cut out 30 circles of pastry and place them onto a baking tray, approximately 1cm apart. Cover tray with plastic wrap and refrigerate for at least 30 minutes.
+ In a small bowl combine egg yolk, water and salt and mix well (this is the glaze for the pastries).
+ On the morning you require puffs, preheat oven to 190°C. Remove plastic wrap from tray and brush glaze onto pastry, being careful not to let glaze run over edges. Sprinkle pastry with poppyseeds and bake for 8–10 minutes or until golden brown and cooked through. Allow pastries to cool.
+ Once cool, split pastries in half horizontally and spread 'bottoms' with Sun-dried Tomato Pesto. Replace tops and arrange pastries on a tray. Cover tray with plastic wrap and refrigerate until required.
+ At point of service, place pastries in a preheated oven (170°C) for 5–6 minutes or until heated through.

SUN-DRIED TOMATO PESTO

The Cheddar cheese in this recipe ensures the firm pesto you need to fill The Widow's Puffs. Oil from sun-dried tomatoes can be used to moisten pesto or retained to use in a vinaigrette. Sun-dried Tomato Pesto can be stored in the refrigerator for up to two weeks or frozen for up to six months.

100g (⅔ cup) sun-dried tomatoes in oil
   (drained and roughly chopped)
75g (¾ cup) grated Parmesan cheese
75g (¾ cup) grated tasty Cheddar cheese
juice of 1 lemon
freshly ground black pepper
¼ cup roughly chopped Italian parsley

+ Using a food processor fitted with a metal blade, process all ingredients (except parsley) until a thick paste is formed.
+ Add parsley and pulse just to combine.
+ Store mixture in an airtight container in refrigerator until required.

SKEWERED GARLIC MUSHROOMS

Absolutely divine with field mushrooms if you are lucky enough to find them.

←
Skewered Garlic Mushrooms

MAKES 24 PASSAROUNDS

1 recipe Garlic Butter (below)
24 baby button mushrooms (washed and dried)
3 slices white sandwich bread (crusts cut off)
Maldon sea salt and freshly ground black pepper
24 Italian parsley leaves

+ Preheat oven to 220°C.
+ Melt 2 tblsp garlic butter in a frypan, add mushrooms and lightly cook until golden brown but not totally cooked through. Cool.
+ Cut each slice of bread in half and then each half into quarters (you should end up with 8 rectangles about 5 x 2½cm). Fold bread rectangles in half and thread each onto a medium wooden skewer followed by a mushroom. Continue skewering until all bread and mushrooms are on skewers.
+ Melt remaining garlic butter. Dip each skewer into garlic butter and place skewers on a low-sided baking tray. Roast for 5–7 minutes or until golden brown.
+ Season with salt and pepper and put a parsley leaf onto each skewer tip. Serve hot.

GARLIC BUTTER

MAKES APPROXIMATELY 125G

100g butter (diced)
30g (8 cloves) garlic (peeled and finely chopped)
Maldon sea salt and freshly ground black pepper
balsamic vinegar to taste if you wish

+ Melt 30g (2 tblsp) butter in a heavy-based frypan. Add garlic and cook until soft and aromatic (do not allow the garlic to brown). Remove garlic from the pan and chill.
+ Soften remaining butter and place into a food processor fitted with a metal blade. Process until smooth and creamy. Add cooked garlic, salt and pepper and process until combined. Season to taste with balsamic vinegar if you wish. Refrigerate until required.

RACLETTE CRISPS

A teflon sheet on the baking tray will make your life easier when you make these. Raclette is a strong-smelling Swiss cheese that melts brilliantly. Don't waste any offcuts. Try grilling leftover Raclette over jacket-baked potatoes and serve with small crispy gherkins.

→
Raclette Crisps

MAKES 16 PASSAROUNDS

250g Raclette cheese
40g basil leaves (roughly chopped)
16 sun-dried tomato halves (finely chopped)
20g (80) pinenuts

+   Preheat oven to 180°C.
+   Slice the cheese into 5–7mm thick slices.
+   Using a 4.5cm round cookie cutter, cut cheese slices into 16 rounds.
+   Place each round 5cm apart on a sprayed baking tray. In the centre of each round place some basil. Place some sun-dried tomato halves on top of the basil and push some pinenuts into the sun-dried tomato.
+   Bake for 12–15 minutes or until the oil bubbles from the cheese (If you let the cheese brown it will be bitter).
+   Cool the crisps on the baking tray and remove with a metal spatula.
+   Serve at room temperature or store in an airtight container.

GOUGÈRES

Do not be put off by the large yield – freeze what you don't use. Particularly appreciated if you serve them with champagne.

Gougères

MAKES 70 PASSAROUNDS

250ml (1 cup) water
70g (7 tblsp) butter
1½ tsp Maldon sea salt
pinch sugar
175g (1¼ cups) flour
4–5 eggs
125g (1¼ cups) grated Gruyère cheese
freshly ground white pepper

+ Preheat oven to 230°C.
+ In a medium saucepan combine water, butter, salt and sugar and bring to the boil.
+ Add flour all at once, then reduce heat to medium. Stir with a wooden spoon for 2 minutes or until the mixture forms a ball, and excess moisture has evaporated.
+ Transfer mixture to an electric mixer fitted with a 'K' beater and beat for 30 seconds until mixture has cooled slightly. Add 4 eggs and continue to beat until combined and mixture has a smooth silky texture. The batter should form a peak with a tip that falls over. If it is too stiff add the white of the remaining egg; if still too stiff add the yolk.
+ Mix in 75g (¾ cup) of cheese and white pepper to taste.
+ Fit a piping bag with a 7mm nozzle and fill with batter.
+ Pipe batter into mounds onto prepared baking tray (each mound about 3cm in diameter). Alternatively, put teaspoons of mixture onto the tray.
+ Sprinkle tops with remaining cheese.
+ Bake 7–8 minutes. Reduce temperature to 180°C and bake a further 15–20 minutes. When Gougères are cooked they will be light golden and slightly moist on the inside.
+ Serve hot or warm.

LUNCH

For most of us during the week 'lunch' is a sammy on the run, but on the weekends you can take time to cook a really fabulous lunch and enjoy it with friends.

MINTED SUMMER PASTA AND
POTATOES

**Minted Summer
Pasta and Potatoes**

This recipe is quick and simple, but relies on all the ingredients being ready at the same time. Timing is important. It's the perfect dish to serve with a newly released Marlborough sauvignon blanc.

2½ tsp salt
500g (1 packet) orecchiette
   (shell-shaped pasta)
500g Jersey Benne potatoes (the
   smallest available) (washed)
500g (2 bunches) asparagus (pinged
   and halved)
250g cows' milk feta cheese (cut into
   1cm squares)
¼ cup roughly chopped mint
65ml (¼ cup) lemon-infused extra
   virgin olive oil
Maldon sea salt and freshly ground
   black pepper

Bring a large pot of water to a rolling boil. Add 1 tsp salt and pasta and cook until pasta is al dente. Drain pasta and retain about ½ cup of cooking water.
While pasta is cooking, bring a small pot of water to a rolling boil and add second teaspoon of salt and potatoes, and cook until soft. Drain potatoes and keep warm.
While pasta and potatoes are cooking, bring a pot of water to a rolling boil, add ½ tsp salt and cook asparagus until al dente. Drain.
In a large serving bowl gently combine pasta, potatoes, asparagus, feta cheese, mint and oil. Season with salt and pepper, and moisten with some of the retained pasta cooking water if desired.
Serve hot, warm or cold.

WARM ASIAN SCALLOP SALAD

Serve in Chinese rice bowls with soup spoons and accompany with a spicy, aromatic Gewürztraminer.

Warm Asian
Scallop Salad

15ml (1 tblsp) olive oil
50g (¼) onion (finely chopped)
thumbnail-sized piece ginger (peeled
    and julienned)
½ small chilli (deseeded and thinly sliced)
375ml (1½ cups) fish stock (preferably
    home-made)
15ml (1 tblsp) medium sherry
230g (20) scallops
4 wonton wrappers
¼ iceberg lettuce (shredded)
4 small spring onions (sliced diagonally
    into 1cm lengths)

Have 4 Chinese rice bowls at the ready.
Heat oil in a small pot. Add onion, ginger and
chilli and cook for 2–3 minutes until soft but
not brown.
Add fish stock and sherry, bring to the boil
and decrease heat so liquid is simmering.
Add scallops and poach for 2–3 minutes,
or until just opaque. Remove scallops to a
warmed plate and cover to keep warm.
One at a time, cook the wonton wrappers in
the simmering liquid for 1–2 minutes or until
al dente. As each wonton wrapper is cooked,
remove and place into a rice bowl.
Add spring onions to simmering liquid and
very briefly warm through.
Place a handful of lettuce onto each wonton
wrapper and arrange 5 scallops on top.
Divide up liquid between bowls and pour
over scallops. Garnish with spring onions.

**Baguette with
Hot-smoked Salmon,
Cucumber Ricotta
and Dill**

BAGUETTE WITH HOT-SMOKED SALMON, CUCUMBER RICOTTA AND DILL

This sandwich is a meal in itself. You can make it ahead to take to a picnic or serve it for a very easy lunch with a bowl of cherry tomatoes and a jar of Aromatic Salt (see page 76).

SERVES 6

1 55–60cm baguette
4 handfuls of lettuce or rocket
1 recipe Cucumber Ricotta (below)
300g hot-smoked salmon
juice of 1 lemon
freshly ground black pepper
8 small spring onions (ends trimmed)
extra virgin olive oil

Cut baguette on the top, lengthways down the centre without cutting all the way through.

Arrange lettuce leaves decoratively along baguette so leaves protrude a little. Push Cucumber Ricotta into centre of baguette, leaving lettuce edges showing.

Top with generous flakes of hot-smoked salmon.

Drizzle salmon with lemon juice and season with pepper.

Lay spring onions lengthways along top of baguette.

Wrap 8 pieces of folded wax paper at even intervals along baguette. Tie each piece with string.

To serve:
Cut between wax paper into even-sized pieces and drizzle salmon with extra virgin olive oil if you wish.

CUCUMBER RICOTTA

MAKES APPROXIMATELY 200g

2–3 Preserved Lemons (see page 58)
125g (½ cup) ricotta
130g (¼ medium) cucumber (cut into 7mm dice)
2 tblsp roughly chopped dill
juice of 1 lemon
Maldon sea salt and freshly ground black pepper to season

Remove pulp from preserved lemons and discard pulp. Rinse skins in cold water, dry on paper towels and finely chop.

Combine all ingredients in a non-reactive bowl and mix well.

Store Cucumber Ricotta in an airtight container in refrigerator until required.

PRESERVED LEMONS

Use chopped preserved lemon rind as a flavour enhancer to salad, pasta or fish dishes. Make sure you lift the lemons out of the jar with tongs. And it is important that the lemons are always submerged under the liquid. To use the lemons, remove from the brine and discard the pulp. Wash the peel and use. Some white crystals will form on the top of the lemons in the jar, which is normal so do not discard the lemons.

Preserved Lemons

MAKES A 1-LITRE JAR

8 lemons
½ cup salt
1 cinnamon stick
4 bay leaves
freshly squeezed lemon juice (as needed)

Cut each lemon into quarters from the top to within 5mm of the bottom, leaving the 4 pieces joined at the stem end. Sprinkle the inside of the lemon with salt.

Place 1 tblsp salt on the bottom of a preserving jar and pack the lemons into the jar, pushing them down and adding more salt as you go.

Push the cinnamon sticks and bay leaves between the lemons.

If the level of the lemon juice doesn't come to the top of the jar, add extra freshly squeezed juice to almost the top of the jar. Leave some airspace before closing the jar.

Let the lemons sit for 1 month, turning the jar upside-down periodically to distribute the salt and juices. Once opened store in the fridge.

Elaine's Spinach
Salad with Verjuice
Vinaigrette

We call this style of salad a 'dump' salad because all you do is chop the ingredients and dump them into a bowl. The ingredients are only a guide – use whatever is available at the market. This recipe began when Elaine made lunch for the staff one day and used up what she found in the chiller.

SERVES 8

1 small red onion (peeled and chopped)
¼ cucumber (peeled and deseeded)
3 tomatoes (chopped)
rind of 1 Preserved Lemon (chopped)
   (see page 58)
1 handful Italian parsley (chopped)
1 avocado (peeled and diced)
6 spring onions (chopped)
350–500g baby spinach
Verjuice Vinaigrette (below)

Combine all ingredients (except spinach and vinaigrette) in a serving bowl and toss together. Scatter spinach on top.
Just before serving, add enough vinaigrette to coat the ingredients and toss together.

MAKES 250ML

3 shallots (peeled and finely diced)
15ml (1 tblsp) lemon juice (approx.
   ½ lemon)
45ml (3 tblsp) white verjuice
125ml (½ cup) extra virgin olive oil
2 tblsp roughly chopped coriander
Maldon sea salt and freshly ground
   black pepper

Macerate shallots in lemon juice, verjuice and a good pinch of salt for 10 minutes.
Whisk in olive oil. Add coriander to taste and season.

COQ-AU-VIN PIE

This pie is very good with mashed potatoes. We also make smaller versions of it in aluminium foil pie-cases.

SERVES 8–9

1.15kg chicken thigh meat (skinned and diced)
butter for sautéing
450g (3 medium) onions (peeled and finely diced)
6 cloves garlic (peeled and finely chopped)
225g rindless bacon (diced)
300g button mushrooms (sliced)
250ml (1 cup) red wine
60g (4 tblsp) butter
60g flour
150ml chicken stock
150ml beef stock
½ cup chopped parsley
bay leaf, sprig of rosemary
Maldon sea salt and freshly ground black pepper
275g puff pastry
1 egg (separated)
1 tblsp water

Preheat oven to 150ºC. Place diced chicken in a casserole dish.

In a heavy frypan melt a little butter and sauté the onion and garlic over a medium heat until it is lightly browned. Transfer onion and garlic to a casserole dish.

Melt a little more butter in the pan and add bacon. Cook until lightly browned. Transfer bacon to the casserole dish. Sauté mushrooms until soft (adding more butter as necessary) and add to casserole.

De-glaze the frypan with red wine and reduce wine by two-thirds. Add wine to casserole.

Melt 60g butter in a small saucepan. Add flour and cook for 2–3 minutes without colouring. Lower temperature and slowly add stock, stirring as you add. Bring sauce to the boil and add to the chicken mixture, along with the herbs and seasoning. Stir to combine. Cover casserole and bake for 35–45 minutes or until chicken is cooked. Pour chicken mixture into the pie dish you will be using and cool as quickly as possible.

Roll out pastry to 2mm thick. Cut out a piece of pastry slightly larger than the pie dish and drape over the chicken mixture. Trim edges.

To decorate the pie lid and bake the pie:

Whisk the egg white until it falls freely from a fork. Brush the edge of the pie pastry with egg white.

Insert a pie funnel into the pie. (Alternatively, make a vent for the pie out of tin foil. Cut a hole in the lid of the pie, large enough to insert the vent. Cut an 8 x 4cm piece of pastry from the leftover pastry, and wrap around the inserted tin foil. Brush on egg white to join the seam.)

Cut the remaining pastry into 2cm thick strips and place a frill around the edge of the pie. You can decorate the pie with leaves cut from the pastry offcuts. Rest pie for at least 30 minutes in the fridge. Preheat oven to 200ºC. Whisk the egg yolk and water together and brush the pie with the glaze. Cut 3 slits in each end of the pie and bake for 30 minutes or until pastry is golden brown.

While the pie is still warm, remove tin foil vent (if using pie funnel leave in). Coq-au-vin Pie can be served immediately or reheated.

Roasted Vegetable Galettes

One of our all-time favourite recipes. We often freeze the galettes totally made up but unbaked, and then bake them from frozen as we need them.

750g puff pastry
your choice of vegetables but here are
    some suggestions:
1 red onion (peeled and sliced)
2 shallots (peeled and sliced)
200g mushrooms (sliced)
2 red peppers (deseeded and sliced)
200g pumpkin (peeled and sliced)
100g zucchinis (diced)
200g kumara (peeled and diced)
olive oil to toss vegetables in
125g (½ cup) blue cheese (chopped)
125g (½ cup) cream cheese
1 egg
1 tblsp finely grated Parmesan cheese
Maldon sea salt and freshly ground
    black pepper
2 eggs (separated)

Roll out pastry and cut into 10 15cm circles.
Place pastry rounds on a greased baking tray
and rest in fridge for at least 20 minutes.
Heat oven to 250°C.
Toss prepared vegetables in a little olive oil
and spread them on a low-sided baking tray.
Hot-roast vegetables in oven for 5–10
minutes until they are soft and golden.
Cool vegetables.
Turn oven to 210°C.
Combine blue cheese, cream cheese, egg
and Parmesan and season with salt and
pepper. Spread onto pastry circles, leaving
a 2.5cm border. Pile roasted vegetables on
top of blue cheese mix.
Lightly whisk egg whites with a fork and
paint pastry borders with egg white wash.
Bring in pastry border to partially cover
vegetables and crimp the border.
Lightly whisk egg yolks with a fork and paint
egg yolk wash onto pastry crimping.
Bake galettes for 30–35 minutes, or until
pastry is golden brown.
Serve hot, warm or at room temperature.

LAMB'S FRY WITH BACON AND APPLE IN SHERRY HONEY GLAZE

Lamb's fry is a very underrated product these days. However, it is very good for the budget and your health. Even non-lamb's fry eaters usually love this dish.

Lamb's Fry with Bacon and Apple in Sherry Honey Glaze

SERVES 4–6

70g (½ cup) flour
15g (1 tblsp) dry mustard
Maldon sea salt and freshly ground
    black pepper
200g (8) bacon rashers
250g lamb's fry (skinned, sliced and
    soaked for a few hours or overnight
    in milk)
45g (3 tblsp) butter
1 Braeburn apple (cored and sliced)
125ml (½ cup) medium sherry
30ml (2 tblsp) liquid honey

Mix together flour, mustard and salt and pepper in a bowl.

Grill bacon until crispy on both sides. Keep warm.

Drain lamb's fry and dry between paper towels. Dredge in flour mixture and dust off excess.

Melt butter in a large frypan and quickly cook lamb's fry in batches on both sides. Reserve and keep warm.

Quickly cook apple in the same pan. Pour sherry into pan, add honey and bring to the boil. Reduce heat until a glaze is achieved. Season to taste.

To serve:
Place a piece of lamb's fry onto a warm plate, add a piece of apple, followed by a bacon rasher. Repeat the process, finishing with a piece of lamb's fry, then pour over glaze.

**Herbed Mussels with
Soused Red Onion**

Mussels are New Zealand's most affordable delicacy. Prepare this dish in a pot or wok on your barbecue in front of guests.

800g–1kg live Greenshell mussels
500ml (2 cups) dry white wine
1 large red onion (peeled and sliced)
2 garlic cloves (peeled and finely
   chopped)
¼ tsp Maldon sea salt
2 tblsp chopped Italian parsley
2 tblsp chopped chervil or dill
45g (3 tblsp) butter (diced)
freshly ground black pepper

Wash mussels under cold running water. Remove beards (strings that hang from the mussels' shells) and discard.
In a heavy-based, wide saucepan or non-reactive wok combine wine, red onion, garlic and salt. Simmer for 5 minutes to slightly cook red onion and garlic.
Add mussels, cover and cook until all mussels are open. This may take 15–20 minutes.
Stir in herbs, butter and pepper.
Serve in soup bowls with lots of the juice, all of the onion and with big cloth napkins for each guest.

CHILLED GAZPACHO WITH PRAWNS AND AVOCADO

Gazpacho is a traditional Spanish peasant dish concocted to use up leftover bread. It's one of my favourite summer dishes.

SERVES 10/MAKES 2.6L

1.5kg ripe tomatoes (roughly chopped)
200g (½ large) cucumber (peeled and finely diced)
150g (1 large) red pepper (deseeded and finely diced)
2 cloves garlic (peeled and finely chopped)
100g crustless Ciabatta bread (broken into chunks)
500ml (2 cups) cold water
1 tblsp Maldon sea salt
freshly ground black pepper
125ml (½ cup) sherry vinegar
125ml (½ cup) extra virgin olive oil
5 tomatoes to garnish
2½ avocados (peeled and stoned)
lemon juice for sprinkling over avocados
30 hot-roasted prawns (below)
basil to garnish

Place tomatoes, cucumber, red pepper, garlic and Ciabatta into a food processor fitted with a metal blade. Pulse briefly to just combine. Stir in water, salt, pepper and vinegar. Refrigerate for at least 1 hour for bread to swell and flavours to blend.
Just before serving, stir in extra virgin olive oil and taste for seasoning (the soup should have quite a tang to it).

To serve:
Cut each tomato in half through the waist and remove the seeds to create a neat shell. Slice each avocado half in 2 (i.e. quarters). Sprinkle avocado with lemon juice.
Ladle 250ml of Gazpacho into each soup bowl. Place a tomato shell in the centre of the soup. Arrange a piece of avocado on either side of the tomato.
Place prawns in the tomato shell and garnish soup with a sprig of basil.

HOT-ROASTED PRAWNS

olive oil
30 prawns
Maldon sea salt and freshly ground black pepper

Preheat oven to 220ºC.
Lightly brush a low-sided roasting tray with olive oil and toss prawns onto tray.
Season prawns with salt and pepper, and roast for 3–5 minutes or until prawns are orange in colour.
Remove prawns from tray and allow to cool. If you choose to cook prawns in advance, refrigerate them until required.

SKEWERED LAMB WITH BOCCONCINI CENTRES

Skewered Lamb with Bocconcini Centres

The better the quality of the lamb mince, the tastier this dish will be. We like to mince lamb leg or lamb rump. Serve with a warm orzo salad, or minted and buttered boiled potatoes.

SERVES 8

480g lamb mince
80g (13–16) sun-dried tomatoes (finely chopped)
3 cloves garlic (finely chopped)
¾ Preserved Lemon (rind only, washed and finely chopped) (see page 58)
15ml (1 tblsp) olive oil
3 tblsp finely chopped Italian parsley
1½ tsp finely chopped savory
1½ tsp Maldon sea salt
¾ tsp freshly ground black pepper
75g (3) Bocconcini balls
olive oil for shallow frying
250g (24) cherry tomatoes
24 basil leaves

In a bowl combine the lamb mince, sun-dried tomatoes, garlic, preserved lemon rind, olive oil, parsley, savory and seasoning.

Divide the mixture into 24 even portions (about 25g), and cut Bocconcini into 24 equal pieces (about 3g each).

Taking one portion of the lamb mixture, flatten it out and place one piece of Bocconcini in the centre. Wrap the lamb around the cheese and roll into an even-shaped ball.

Using a heavy-based frypan heat enough oil in the base to enable you to shallow fry. Cook balls over medium heat, rolling them around to ensure even cooking. This will take about 5 minutes.

Remove from heat and place onto paper towels. Cover with a clean tea towel to keep warm.

Into the same hot frypan place the cherry tomatoes and cook over a low heat until just warmed through.

Carefully skewer a lamb ball, followed by a basil leaf and a tomato. Repeat this sequence, finishing with a third tomato. Serve hot or warm.

ANTIPASTO

Antipasto can be the entrée before the main
course or a snack in the late afternoon, or
for any time you have friends around. Plattered
food is easy on the cook, and guests just
love passing and sharing food.

AROMATIC SALT

Perfect with hard-boiled eggs, cherry tomatoes or steamed and peeled new potatoes. Also delicious on grilled lamb chops or fish.

→
Aromatic Salt

YIELDS ¾ CUP/120G

100g Maldon sea salt
½ cinnamon quill
1 tsp (18) whole allspice
½ tsp fenugreek seeds
1 tsp dried mint
15g (1 tblsp) whole blanched almonds
½ tsp turmeric

+ Grind all ingredients in a mortar with a pestle.
+ Store in screw-top jars.

ROASTED ALMONDS WITH PAPRIKA

Add bowls of these with some pimento-stuffed olives to your antipasto table.

YIELDS 250G

**250g (1¾ cups) blanched almonds
1 tsp olive oil
1 tsp smoked paprika
1½ tsp finely ground Maldon sea salt**

+ Preheat oven to 150°C.
+ Place almonds on a baking tray and dry roast in the top of the oven for 25 minutes or until golden brown.
+ Remove from oven and stir in the olive oil, paprika and salt.
+ Return to oven for a further 2–3 minutes.
+ Remove from oven and cool. Store in an airtight container.

MINTED PEA DIP

Serve this colourful dip with barbecued bruschetta or use it in a sandwich with leftover lamb for a taste sensation.

YIELDS 470G/2 CUPS

**500g (3¾ cups) frozen minted peas
1 tsp Maldon sea salt
½ tsp freshly ground black pepper
60ml (¼ cup) olive oil
¼ cup chopped mint**

+ In a pot of boiling salted water blanch peas, then refresh.
+ Transfer peas to food processor and process for 30 seconds until mushy but not smooth.
+ Add seasoning, and with processor running pour oil slowly through feed tube.
+ Remove pea purée to a bowl and stir in mint. Taste for seasoning and serve warm or cold.

CARROT AND CUMIN DIP

Serve a bowl of this alongside Minted Pea Dip. If you wish accompany with shaved Parmesan or crisped prosciutto crumbled on top.

MAKES 465G/2 CUPS

**1kg (10–12) carrots (peeled and
    roughly chopped)
1 tblsp cumin seeds
30ml (2 tblsp) olive oil
1 tsp Maldon sea salt
½ tsp freshly ground black pepper
45ml (3 tblsp) tahini
15ml (1 tblsp) olive oil
10ml (2 tsp) lime juice
extra salt and pepper if necessary**

+ Preheat oven to 190°C.
+ Toss together carrots, cumin seeds, oil and salt and pepper and place on a low-sided baking tray.
+ Place tray in oven and cook for 25–35 minutes, or until carrots are soft. Remove from oven and cool.
+ Place carrots in a food processor fitted with metal blade and process until smooth.
+ Add tahini, olive oil and lime juice. Pulse to combine.
+ Season to taste.

SEMI-DRIED TOMATOES

Toss these warm through freshly cooked, dried pasta or serve on grilled zucchini topped with Marinated Cows' Milk Feta (see page 83) or just pile on a big platter so guests can squash them onto bruschetta.

→
Semi-dried Tomatoes

YIELDS 24–36 TOMATO HALVES

**1–1.5kg (14–20) tomatoes
   (preferably plum tomatoes)
3 tblsp extra virgin olive oil
Maldon sea salt and freshly
   ground black pepper
basil (optional)**

+ Preheat oven to 150ºC.
+ Halve tomatoes lengthways and place cut side up on a non-reactive deep roasting tray.
+ Sprinkle tomatoes with olive oil and salt and pepper.
+ Bake in oven for 2 hours or until tomatoes are shrivelled and almost pasty.
+ Serve hot, warm or cold, preferably with fresh basil.

BARBECUED BRUSCHETTA

(25–30 SLICES)

**1 baguette
100ml (⅓ cup plus 1 tblsp) olive oil**

+ Cut baguette into diagonal slices about 1.5–2cm thick. Brush each slice on both sides with olive oil.
+ Place on a heated barbecue flat plate and cook on each side for 20–30 seconds, or until golden and crisp.

WARM LENTIL SALAD WITH MARINATED COWS' MILK FETA

This salad is absolutely divine poked into warm pita breads. I had an aversion to lentils based on a prejudice from the 1970s, but green Puy lentils won me over.

←

Warm Lentil Salad
with Marinated
Cows' Milk Feta

SERVES 8

210g (1 cup) Puy lentils
750ml (3 cups) water
1 small red pepper
1 small yellow pepper
½–¾ tsp Maldon sea salt and freshly
    ground black pepper
olive oil
2 garlic cloves (crushed)
1 thumbnail-sized piece fresh ginger
    (peeled and very finely chopped)
1 tsp ground cumin
¼ tsp ground coriander
75ml (5 tblsp) olive oil
30ml (2 tblsp) red wine vinegar
¼ cup roughly chopped mint
2 tblsp pinenuts (lightly toasted)
100g (7–10) cherry tomatoes (halved)
1 recipe Marinated Cows' Milk Feta
    (below)

+ Place lentils in a medium saucepan and cover with water. Bring to the boil. Turn down heat and simmer until tender (about 25 minutes). Drain well.
+ Preheat oven to 200°C.
+ Cut peppers into 1–1.5cm strips and toss in a little olive oil with salt and pepper. Place peppers onto a baking tray and roast for 7–10 minutes until tender.
+ To cook aromatics: in a small frypan sauté the garlic and ginger in a little oil. Remove pan from heat, add the cumin and coriander and stir well. Set aside.
+ To make the dressing: combine oil, vinegar and mint in the serving bowl.
+ Add lentils, peppers, aromatics, 1 tblsp pinenuts, cherry tomatoes, half recipe of Marinated Feta and seasoning to the bowl and gently combine.
+ Scatter top with the remaining pinenuts and Marinated Feta.

MARINATED COWS' MILK FETA

Sprinkle this into halved potatoes baked in their jackets or put out a bowl of it for guests to spread onto bread.

1 tblsp pinenuts (lightly toasted and
    finely chopped)
2 tblsp finely chopped mint
1 tblsp finely chopped parsley
1 clove garlic (crushed)
30ml (2 tblsp) olive oil
¼ tsp freshly ground black pepper
125g cows' milk feta (diced into
    1–1.5cm squares)

+ In a bowl combine the pinenuts, mint, parsley, garlic, olive oil and pepper.
+ Add the feta and marinate in the refrigerator for at least 1 hour or overnight. It will keep for several days.

ANTIPASTO 84

BEETROOT SALAD

Fresh tarragon makes this salad unique – try it alongside an omelette sprinkled with Aromatic Salt
(see page 76).

Beetroot Salad

SERVES 8

500g beetroot (tops removed)
2 sprigs lemon thyme
65ml (¼ cup) water
125g (1) red onion (thinly sliced)
40g (3 tblsp) capers (rinsed and
    drained)
handful of tarragon leaves
    (roughly chopped)
1 tsp Maldon sea salt
½ tsp freshly ground black pepper
1 recipe Red Wine Vinegar Dressing
    (below)

+ Preheat oven to 200°C.
+ Place beetroot, lemon thyme and water onto
  a square of aluminum foil. (Pull corners of foil
  together to enclose beetroot so the steam
  created is retained.)
+ Roast in oven for 1–1¼ hours until beetroot
  is tender when skewered. (Skewer through
  the foil.) Cool.
+ Peel and slice beetroot into rounds, then
  cut into 5mm matchsticks.
+ In a medium-sized bowl combine the beetroot,
  onions, capers, tarragon and salt and pepper.
+ Pour the dressing over and gently combine
  so all vegetables are coated.
+ The flavour improves if the salad is left for
  an hour or two before serving. Toss again just
  prior to serving.

RED WINE VINEGAR DRESSING

75ml (5 tblsp) olive oil
30ml (2 tblsp) red wine vinegar
2 tblsp Dijon mustard
4–5 sprigs tarragon (finely chopped)
1½ tsp Maldon sea salt
½ tsp freshly ground black pepper

+ In a small bowl combine oil, vinegar, mustard,
  tarragon and salt and pepper. Whisk well with
  a fork.

BARBECUED PITA BREAD

This recipe allows you to make and form Pita Bread and freeze it before baking. One hour before you need to eat, take the dough out of the freezer to defrost and for the second rising, then barbecue.

MAKES 4 185G PITA BREADS

6g (2 tsp) dried yeast
300ml tepid water
pinch sugar
500g flour (bakers' if possible)
½ tsp salt
15ml (1 tblsp) olive oil

+ Dissolve yeast in 50mls of the tepid water. Add sugar and leave in a warm place for about 10 minutes, or until mixture is frothy and bubbly.

+ Sift flour and salt into a mixing bowl. Make a well in the centre and pour in the yeast mixture.

+ Knead mixture by hand for 10–12 minutes, adding enough of the remaining water and oil to make a soft but not wet dough. (Alternatively, place in an electric mixer bowl with a dough hook fitted. Add water and oil, and knead for 5–8 minutes until dough is soft but not wet.)

+ Rub the base of a large bowl with a little oil. Roll dough round and round in the bowl to grease all over. Leave dough in bowl. Cover with a damp cloth and leave in a warm place for 1½–2 hours until nearly doubled in size.

+ Punch the dough down and knead again for a few minutes. Divide dough into 4 balls.

+ Using a rolling pin, roll out each ball into a circle approximately 1cm thick and 17cm in diameter. (If you wish to freeze for later, do so at this stage on a greased tray.)

+ Place onto lightly dusted tea towels and cover. Leave to prove until double in size.

+ Preheat barbecue flat plate until hot. We place teflon sheets on heated barbecue plate and then place pita breads onto teflon and cook 3–4 minutes on each side, or until light golden in colour.

+ If baking in the oven, preheat oven to 180°C. Preheat a lightly oiled baking tray for 1–2 minutes. Remove tray from oven and place pita breads on tray. Sprinkle the breads with water and quickly place in oven. Bake for 6–10 minutes.

+ Wrap pita bread in tea towels to keep warm until ready to serve.

JEWELLED SALMON GRAVLAX

Traditional gravlax is sides of salmon cured with salt, sugar and dill, then sliced very thinly. This is my fast-track version imitating a method I saw Jacques Pepin demonstrate. I now prefer this recipe to the traditional version. I particularly like the coloured garnish.

→
**Jewelled Salmon
Gravlax**

10 ENTRÉE SERVES

1¼ tsp Maldon sea salt
½ tsp freshly ground black pepper
500g salmon fillet (sliced very finely
   on an angle)
juice from 1 orange (warmed)
45g (⅓ cup) dried cranberries
20g (2 tblsp) capers (drained)
20g (2 tblsp) finely chopped red onion
20g (2 tblsp) finely chopped shallots
2 tblsp mixed fresh herbs (tarragon,
   parsley and chives combined)
30ml (2 tblsp) extra virgin olive oil
2–3 lemons (cut into wedges)

+ Sprinkle ½ tsp of the salt and the pepper onto a serving platter.
+ Taking care not to disturb the seasonings, arrange the salmon slices side by side on the platter without overlapping. Sprinkle the remaining salt evenly over the salmon and cover with plastic wrap. Set aside for at least 30 minutes to cure at room temperature, or if you wish, refrigerate for up to one day.
+ Pour orange juice over the cranberries and set aside to cool. Drain and reserve any juice for another use.
+ Sprinkle the salmon with capers, red onion, shallots, cranberries and herbs, then drizzle with extra virgin olive oil.
+ Serve at room temperature with lemon wedges.

Roast Rack of
Pork with Trivet
Potatoes, Apple and
Calvados Sauce and
Old-fashioned Gravy

recipe page 92

DINNER

Your house is the perfect place to dine. Rather than
meeting friends out, invite them over for dinner. Take
your time to lay the table, arrange flowers, work out
what wine you will serve and where you will have
pre-dinner drinks – enjoy the preparation.

ROAST RACK OF PORK WITH TRIVET POTATOES, APPLE AND CALVADOS SAUCE AND OLD-FASHIONED GRAVY

This is a magnificent version of a roast dinner, which is sometimes the perfect way to entertain. Ask your butcher for female pork as it never seems to have the strong odour often associated with pork (see picture page 90).

SERVES 8

1 tblsp olive oil plus extra for
  greasing tray
1.5kg potatoes (preferably Agria)
1.5kg (8 rib) rack of pork with the
  rind intact
190ml (¾ cup) dry white wine
315ml (1¼ cups) chicken stock
1 tblsp Maldon sea salt (crushed)
1 recipe Apple and Calvados Sauce
  (opposite)
1 recipe Old-fashioned Gravy
  (opposite)

Preheat oven to 200ºC. Brush a non-reactive roasting tray with olive oil. Cut potatoes into 1cm thick slices and place in the base of the tray. These become a trivet for the pork. Score the rind of the pork (make 5mm incisions in the pork rind, ensuring the cuts extend to the base, to allow the rendered fat to run freely into the pan) and place the pork rack on top of the potatoes in the tray (so that the crackling is exposed). Pour the wine and chicken stock over the pork and potatoes. Brush the pork rind and exposed flesh with olive oil and rub in the salt, smearing it well into the cuts.

Roast for 30 minutes on the top shelf of the oven, until the sides of the crackling have started to crisp.

Reduce heat to 180ºC and cook for a further 1–1¼ hours or until the juices run clear when a skewer is inserted. (If the crackling is not sufficiently crisp, give it another 10 minutes on 200ºC.) Transfer pork to a clean tray and leave to rest in a warm place for 10 minutes, covered with aluminium foil. Turn the oven off and leave the potatoes in the oven to keep warm and crisp.

Serve Roast Pork and Trivet Potatoes with Apple and Calvados Sauce and Old-fashioned Gravy.

APPLE AND CALVADOS SAUCE

Calvados is an apple brandy made in Calvados, Normandy, France. Granny Smith apples are the best sauce apples as they become almost creamy with cooking. This sauce can be frozen.

MAKES 375ML/1½ CUPS

3 (about 500g) Granny Smith apples
  (peeled and cored)
30ml (2 tblsp) Calvados
1 cinnamon stick
15g (1 tblsp) sugar
250ml (1 cup) water
½ tsp freshly grated nutmeg
Maldon sea salt and freshly ground
  black pepper

Roughly chop apples and place in a non-reactive pot.
Add Calvados, cinnamon stick, sugar and water and bring to the boil.
Simmer for 8–10 minutes, stirring occasionally, until the apples are soft and the juices have evaporated.
Beat with a wooden spoon until smooth. Add nutmeg and season to taste. Serve warm.

OLD-FASHIONED GRAVY

You can make this gravy ahead and freeze. It's possibly not as tasty as gravy made from scrapings in the roasting pan, but it does cut down on the stress of last-minute preparation. If you have meat juices from a previous roast, use 1 tblsp meat juice in place of the Vegemite or Marmite.

MAKES 500ML/2 CUPS

30g (2 tblsp) butter
2 tblsp flour
1 tsp Vegemite or Marmite
750ml (3 cups) chicken stock (hot)
3 sprigs rosemary
Maldon sea salt and freshly ground
  black pepper

In a small saucepan melt the butter until sizzling. Sprinkle the flour over the top and quickly stir with a wooden spoon to combine. Reduce heat and gently cook the flour for 3–4 minutes, stirring almost constantly to prevent the flour from overcooking.
Add the Vegemite and stir through.
Gradually pour in the chicken stock, stirring continuously until all the stock has been added. Add the rosemary, season and simmer for 10 minutes. Strain and serve hot.

**Groper Steaks with
Tomato and
Cucumber Salad**

GROPER STEAKS WITH TOMATO
AND CUCUMBER SALAD

Groper, also known as hapuka, is a member of the bass family and is a very firm, tasty fish. This is such a simple dish, but it is always effective. Crusty bread is the perfect starch to serve with this meal.

olive oil
4 groper steaks
Maldon sea salt
Tomato and Cucumber Salad (below)
2 lemons

Heat a heavy-bottomed frypan and smear with olive oil. Sear groper steaks on each side until cooked. Depending on thickness of groper steaks, it may take 5 minutes per side. Sprinkle with salt. You may need to cook the steaks 2 at a time. If so, place the first 2 cooked groper steaks on a warmed plate and cover with a tea towel.
Divide Tomato and Cucumber Salad between plates and place groper steak on serving plate next to salad. Accompany each serve with a lemon half.

TOMATO AND CUCUMBER SALAD

This is a 'dump' salad because you dump all the ingredients into a bowl. Make just before you are going to serve it, or while the groper is cooking.

4–6 tomatoes (cored and cut into chunks)
½ medium cucumber (cut into chunks)
10–15 black olives
bunch of mint (roughly chopped)
60ml (¼ cup) extra virgin olive oil
15ml (1 tblsp) balsamic vinegar
Maldon sea salt and freshly ground
   black pepper

Put all ingredients into a bowl and toss together with your hands. Taste for seasoning.

PARMESAN CHICKEN WITH BALSAMIC BUTTER SAUCE

Serve this dish with a mélange of colourful, crunchy vegetables dressed with extra virgin olive oil.

Parmesan Chicken
with Balsamic
Butter Sauce

SERVES 4

500g (8 pieces) chicken thigh (bone out, skin on)
65ml (¼ cup) extra virgin olive oil
50g (½ cup) freshly grated Parmesan cheese
3 tblsp finely chopped oregano
2 cloves garlic (crushed)
Maldon sea salt and freshly ground black pepper
250ml (1 cup) chicken stock
125ml (½ cup) balsamic vinegar
20g (2 tblsp) butter (unsalted and cold)

Preheat oven to 200°C.

In a large bowl toss the chicken with olive oil, Parmesan, oregano and garlic.

Arrange chicken pieces in a roasting tray and season with salt and pepper.

In a saucepan combine chicken stock and vinegar. Boil over high heat until reduced to ⅓ cup (about 10 minutes).

Bake chicken for 15 minutes or until lightly browned and just cooked through. Take out of oven, cover tray with aluminium foil and rest for at least 5 minutes.

Remove saucepan from heat and whisk in butter, 1 tablespoon at a time, until smooth. Season with salt and pepper.

Transfer chicken to plates, spoon sauce over top and serve.

**Whole Fish with
Roasted Red Pepper
and Basil Butter**

Barbecue all year round – it is a convenient way to cook.

1 (700–800g) whole fish (gutted)
1 recipe Roasted Red Pepper and Basil
   Butter (below)
1 lemon (cut into wedges)
small bunch basil
125ml (½ cup) white wine
12 black olives
Maldon sea salt and freshly ground
   black pepper

Preheat barbecue.
Wash fish and trim fins with kitchen scissors.
On both sides of the fish make vertical
incisions to the bone and stud incisions with
lemon wedges (we usually make 5 incisions).
Smear butter all over fish and place basil into
cavity (reserve remaining butter for another use).
Place fish onto a double thickness, large
sheet of aluminium foil. Add wine and olives
and season with salt and pepper. Fold foil so
it becomes a bag for the fish and seal foil.
Cook for about 30 minutes on a medium-
heated barbecue. Check if cooked by
inserting a metal cake skewer into fish
through foil.

115g (1 medium) red pepper (roasted,
   peeled and chopped)
175g butter (diced and softened)
handful of basil (chopped)
Maldon sea salt and freshly ground
   black pepper

Place red pepper and butter into a food
processor and pulse until combined.
Place into a bowl and mix in basil. Season
to taste.

FILLET OF BEEF AND PORTABELLO MUSHROOMS WITH GARLIC AND RED ONION CONSERVE

A whole fillet of beef is the easiest way to entertain because you have minimum effort for maximum appreciation. Seek your butcher's advice and buy the best quality fillet you possibly can.

SERVES 10

1.5–2kg beef fillet (trimmed of silverskin and fat, chain removed by your butcher)
125ml (½ cup) olive oil
freshly ground black pepper
rosemary and bayleaf sprigs
15–20 Portabello mushrooms
olive oil for brushing mushrooms
1 recipe Garlic and Red Onion Conserve (below)

Place beef in a bowl and drizzle with olive oil, then add pepper and herbs. Toss beef to give an even coating of oil. Refrigerate for at least 2 hours, preferably overnight.
Before barbecuing, bring beef back to room temperature.
Preheat barbecue – It needs to be hot. Initially sear beef on all sides and then barbecue for 20–25 minutes (turning once during the cooking time) or until cooked medium rare. Remove beef from barbecue and place in a roasting tray. Cover the tray with a heavy tea towel and rest beef for 10–15 minutes away from the heat.
While beef is resting, brush each mushroom with olive oil and barbecue for around 5 minutes on each side.
Serve beef and mushrooms with Garlic and Red Onion Conserve.

GARLIC AND RED ONION CONSERVE

MAKES 330ML

4 heads of garlic
60ml (4 tblsp) olive oil
45ml (3 tblsp) olive oil
500g (4 medium) red onions (peeled and thinly sliced)
15ml (1 tblsp) balsamic vinegar
5 tblsp chopped thyme
Maldon sea salt and freshly ground black pepper

Preheat oven to 180°C.
Place each garlic head onto a square of aluminium foil, pour 1 tblsp of olive oil over each and wrap up. Roast for 45 minutes or until garlic is soft. Remove and allow to cool to room temperature.
Heat olive oil in a heavy frypan over a medium heat. Add red onions and stir constantly for the first 5 minutes, then cook onions until they become brownish and slightly gooey (this will take about 15 to 20 minutes). Remove onions from heat and set aside.
Cut base off garlic head, squeeze pulp out from cloves and combine it with cooked onions in a food processor. Add balsamic vinegar, thyme and salt and pepper and process until combined.

ROASTED VEGETABLE SALAD

Roasted Vegetable Salad

ROASTED VEGETABLE SALAD

You could barbecue all these vegetables to make a delicious barbecued vegetable salad, but I prefer to roast the vegetables and assemble the salad ahead. You can make it one or two days beforehand as it improves with age!

SERVES 8

about 400g red peppers
about 400g yellow peppers
olive oil for lightly coating vegetables
about 400g eggplant (sliced into
  5mm rounds)
100g (20) garlic cloves (peeled)
about 400g red onion (peeled and
  sliced into 5mm rings)
2½ tblsp balsamic vinegar
Maldon sea salt and freshly ground
  black pepper
Italian parsley or basil leaves for
  garnishing

Preheat oven to 250ºC.
Seed peppers and cut into 1cm strips.
Spray all vegetables with olive oil and place separately onto low-sided bun trays.
Bake peppers for 15 minutes or until soft. Set aside to cool.
Bake garlic for 10 minutes or until lightly browned. Set aside to cool.
Bake red onion and eggplant for 15–20 minutes or until onion is slightly caramelised and eggplant is soft. Set aside to cool.
Remove vegetables from trays and place into a large bowl. Add balsamic vinegar and season to taste.
Place salad on a serving platter and garnish with Italian parsley or basil leaves.

FISH BAKED IN PARCHMENT WITH POTATOES AND ONIONS

Parchment (baking paper) is, of course, inedible. Place kitchen scissors on the table so that guests know to cut the paper.

SERVES 4

olive oil for sautéing
1 medium carrot (thinly sliced)
1 medium onion (thinly sliced)
1 stick celery (thinly sliced)
Potatoes and Onions (below)
4 150g pieces fish (a fleshy fish like groper or bluenose works well)
Maldon sea salt
freshly ground black pepper
4 big sprigs Italian parsley
1 lemon (thinly sliced)
40g butter (melted) for brushing

Preheat oven to 220ºC.

To cut parchment to fit for fish portion: Fold a large piece of parchment paper in half and cut out two ear-shaped pieces so that when the paper is opened out it is heart-shaped. Each half must be wider than the fish fillets at every edge by 7cm. You will need 4 pieces of cut parchment.

Heat a little olive oil in a pan and sauté the carrots, onion and celery until lightly coloured and just tender. Chill.

Divide the Potatoes and Onions recipe between the 4 parcels and top each with carrot, onion and celery.

Place the fish on top of the vegetables and season. Add a big sprig of Italian parsley and a slice of lemon to each parcel.

Brush edges of parchment paper with melted butter, fold paper to enclose fish and make small overlapping folds to seal the edges, starting at the curve of the heart.

Place parcels on a baking sheet and bake for 10–12 minutes or until paper is puffed and fish is opaque.

POTATOES AND ONIONS

MAKES ENOUGH FOR 4 FISH PARCELS

300g waxy potatoes (thinly sliced)
Maldon sea salt
1 tblsp olive oil plus extra for drizzling
1 tblsp water
1 large onion (thinly sliced)
bunch Italian parsley (finely chopped)
freshly ground black pepper

Simmer sliced potatoes in lightly salted water for 4–5 minutes or until just cooked. Refresh under cold water and drain well.

Pour olive oil and water into a frypan and once hot, add onion. Cook until the water has evaporated and the onion starts to colour.

Combine potatoes, onion and parsley.

Season and drizzle with a little olive oil. Chill.

PALEY'S PLACE GRILLED LAMB
CHOPS WITH THREE TOMATO
SALAD

Paley's Place Grilled
Lamb Chops with
Three Tomato Salad

The secret to this dish is the thickness of the chops. You will need to specially request them from your butcher. Paley's Place is a terrific restaurant in Portland, Oregon, where I first tasted double thickness lamb chops.

SERVES 6–12

45ml (3 tblsp) Dijon mustard
7g (2 tsp) crushed garlic
30ml (2 tblsp) balsamic vinegar
½ tsp Maldon sea salt and freshly
   ground black pepper
125ml (½ cup) olive oil
3 tblsp coarsely chopped rosemary
2kg (12) 4cm thick rib lamb chops
1 recipe Three Tomato Salad
   (below)

Combine Dijon mustard, garlic, balsamic vinegar and salt and pepper in a non-reactive bowl. Slowly whisk in olive oil to form a creamy marinade. Stir in the rosemary and add the lamb chops to the marinade. Toss to coat evenly. Cover bowl and marinate chops for 1–3 hours or, better still, overnight.
Preheat grill or barbecue to a high temperature. Grill or barbecue the chops for 4–5 minutes on each side, or until pink and juicy in the centre. Cover chops and rest for 10 minutes. Place chops onto warmed plates with a spoonful of Three Tomato Salad nestled beside each chop.

THREE TOMATO SALAD

Ray McVinnie introduced me to the idea of combining tomatoes in different states in a salad.

70g (½ cup) sun-dried tomatoes in oil
   (sliced)
180g (1 cup) Semi-dried Tomatoes
   (see page 80)
245g (6) large tomatoes (cut into wedges)
50g (½) red onion (sliced)
40g (½ cup) black olives (pitted)
20g (4) anchovies (chopped)
Maldon sea salt and freshly ground
   black pepper
45ml (3 tblsp) extra virgin olive oil

Put the 3 versions of tomatoes, red onion, olives and anchovies into a bowl. Season with salt and pepper. Set aside for 20 minutes. Add olive oil and toss gently to combine.

CORNED BEEF WITH WINTER SALAD AND FEIJOA CHUTNEY

This is the lightened-up version of a traditional winter dish – great presented on a large platter. If you wish, add some small, peeled potatoes during the last thirty minutes of cooking time to serve with the corned beef. Alternatively, serve with mashed potatoes.

Corned Beef with
Winter Salad and
Feijoa Chutney

SERVES 6–8

1.5kg piece of corned beef silverside
  (rinsed)
250g (1 large) onion (peeled and halved)
150g (1 medium) carrot (peeled and
  chopped)
85g (2 stalks) celery (washed and
  chopped)
1 recipe Winter Salad (below)
1 recipe Feijoa Chutney (below)
1 recipe Manuka Honey Mustard Dressing
  (see page 10)

Place silverside in a large pot. Add vegetables and cover with cold water. Bring to the boil and simmer gently with the lid slightly ajar for 90 minutes. Rest meat in cooking liquid for 15–20 minutes.

To serve
Place a portion of Winter Salad in the middle of a plate. Discard pot vegetables, remove beef from the cooking liquid and slice. Place beef over the salad, drizzle over extra dressing, and accompany with Feijoa Chutney.

WINTER SALAD

The finer you slice the vegetables, the more delicious the salad becomes. A chef's tool called a mandoline is excellent for this job.

SERVES 6–8

150g (¼) cabbage (washed and
  very finely sliced)
60g (1 small) carrot (peeled and grated)
100g (2–3) radishes (washed and very
  finely sliced)
Italian parsley (finely chopped)
50g (½ small) red onion (peeled and
  very thinly sliced)
45ml (3 tblsp) Manuka Honey Mustard
  Dressing (see page 10)
Maldon sea salt and freshly ground
  black pepper

In a bowl mix together all the ingredients. Coat with enough dressing to moisten and season to taste.

FEIJOA CHUTNEY

This is from *The Essential Digby Law* published by Hodder Moa Beckett. Feijoas have a short season, so watch out for them.

SERVES 6–8

1kg feijoas
500g onions
300g raisins
500g pitted dates
500g brown sugar
1 tblsp ground ginger
1 tblsp curry powder
1 tsp ground cloves
½ tsp cayenne pepper
4 tsp salt
4 cups malt vinegar

Wipe the feijoas, trim the ends and finely slice. Finely chop onions and coarsely chop raisins and dates. Combine all ingredients in a large saucepan, bring to the boil and cook very gently for 1½–2 hours, or until the chutney is thick. Make sure it doesn't catch on the bottom of the saucepan. Pour into hot clean jars and seal.

**Braised Leeks
with Rosemary**

My friend Sarah Hodge from Horrobin and Hodge, a nursery specialising in culinary herbs, first cooked leeks this way for me. They are very good with roast pork.

SERVES 4

1.5kg (4 medium) leeks
15g (1 tblsp) butter
250ml (1 cup) chicken stock
1 sprig rosemary
30ml (2 tblsp) white wine
Maldon sea salt and freshly ground
    black pepper

Preheat oven to 180°C.
Trim green part off leeks and reserve for another use.
Cut white part of the leek into three or four pieces lengthways.
Melt butter in a casserole over a medium heat and toss leeks around in butter.
Add stock, rosemary, wine and seasoning.
Cover casserole and bake leeks for 40–45 minutes or until leeks are tender.

**Better-than-your-
mother-made
Brussels Sprouts**

People who normally loathe Brussels sprouts love this recipe. The thinner you shred the Brussels sprouts, the better this dish will be. There is a chef's tool called a mandoline, which is perfect for the job. Substitute one small onion for the shallots if you wish.

SERVES 4

30g (2 tblsp) butter
60g (4) shallots (peeled and finely sliced)
4 cloves garlic (peeled and finely
    chopped)
300g (8) Brussels sprouts (washed,
    cored and thinly shredded)
Maldon sea salt and freshly ground
    black pepper
handful Italian parsley (finely chopped)
lemon-infused extra virgin olive oil
    (optional)

In a large frypan heat butter over a medium heat, add shallots and garlic and gently cook until soft but not brown.
Add Brussels sprouts and cook for 4–5 minutes or until sprouts are soft. Season to taste, add parsley, and if you wish dress with lemon-infused extra virgin olive oil.

BEER-BRAISED BEEF WITH PASTRY HAT

You could eliminate the pastry from this recipe and serve the braised beef as a casserole accompanied with mashed potatoes. You will achieve a puffier rise on puff pastry if you place it on the pie upside down from how you cut it.

Beer-braised Beef
with Pastry Hat

SERVES 8

15ml (1 tblsp) olive oil
125g slab bacon (diced)
30ml (2 tblsp) olive oil
1.5kg chuck steak (cut into 60–75g
  pieces)
Maldon sea salt and freshly ground
  black pepper
750g (6 large) onions (peeled and sliced)
30g (2 tblsp) flour
750ml (3 cups) beer
1 bouquet garni (thyme, parsley and
  bayleaves tied)
600–800g pre-rolled puff pastry
1 egg yolk
1 tblsp water

Preheat oven to 160ºC.
Heat first measure of oil in a large casserole dish, add bacon and cook until brown. Remove bacon and set aside. Add second measure of oil, heat, then add beef in batches and seal on both sides. Season the beef, remove and set aside.
Add onions and soften gently over a medium heat. Add flour and mix through the onions. Add beer and remove all the browned bits from the bottom of the casserole with a wooden spoon. Bring the mixture to the boil, add reserved bacon and beef to casserole. Add bouquet garni and season.
Cover casserole with a lid and cook in oven for 4 hours or until the beef is tender. Remove from oven and cool completely. Remove any fat from the top of the mixture. Divide casserole among 8 ovenproof bowls.
Mix egg yolk with water and eggwash rims of the 8 bowls. Roll the pastry to 3mm thickness and cut 8 discs that are 2cm larger in diameter than the size of the bowl. Flip pastry discs over and place on top of bowls.
Preheat oven to 220ºC.
Brush pastry tops with eggwash.
Place in oven and cook for 15–20 minutes until the pastry is brown and puffy.

Duck Shepherd's Pie

This is our version of the signature dish at Balthazar restaurant in Soho, New York. Serve with a mixed green salad. Include some bitter leaves such as rocket, radicchio or endive to help cut back the richness of the pie.

6 duck legs (wild if you wish)
80g (½ cup) onion (peeled and diced)
65g (½ cup) celery (diced)
80g (½ cup) carrot (peeled and diced)
60g (½ cup) celeriac (peeled and diced)
8 cloves garlic (peeled)
5 sprigs thyme
1.5l (2 bottles) cabernet sauvignon
Maldon sea salt and freshly ground
    black pepper
45ml (3 tblsp) olive oil
30g (2 tblsp) tomato paste
30g (2 tblsp) flour
750ml (3 cups) duck stock (or a mixture
    of chicken and beef)
140g (1½ cups) shiitake mushrooms
    (sliced)

700g (4) large potatoes (preferably
    Desirée) (peeled and diced)
180g (1½ cups) celeriac (peeled
    and diced)
400g (3 large) parsnips (peeled
    and diced)
125ml (½ cup) cream
45g (3 tblsp) butter
80g (8 tblsp) finely grated
    Parmesan cheese

Place potatoes, celeriac and parsnips into steamer and cook until soft. Mash until smooth. Add cream and butter, then season to taste.

Trim excess fat from duck legs and place in a large non-reactive dish. Add onion, celery, carrots, celeriac, garlic, thyme and wine. Cover and place in refrigerator overnight to marinate. Remove duck legs from marinade and pat dry with paper towels.

Strain vegetables from marinade and set aside. Reserve marinade. Season duck legs with salt and pepper.

Preheat oven to 185°C.

Heat 1 tblsp of olive oil in a large frypan. Slowly brown duck legs all over. Remove from pan. Discard all but 4 tblsp of duck fat. Transfer vegetables, garlic and thyme from marinade to pan. Sauté over medium heat until browned.

Add tomato paste and flour and cook for 5 minutes. Add reserved marinade and cook until liquid is reduced by two-thirds.

Add stock, bring to the boil and skim. Place duck legs in large casserole dish and cover with sauce (reduced marinade and stock). Cook in oven for about 2½ hours or until duck legs are tender.

Remove duck legs and let them cool slightly. Remove fat from duck legs and shred meat. Reserve sauce and vegetables.

Heat remaining olive oil in large frypan, add mushrooms and cook over a medium heat for 5 minutes.

When you are ready to serve Duck Shepherd's Pie, place duck meat in a large bowl and combine with mushrooms and reserved vegetables. Add enough sauce to moisten the mixture.

Place meat mixture in a large ovenproof gratin dish (or 8 individual gratin dishes). Cover with Potato Topping and sprinkle with Parmesan cheese.

Preheat oven to 200°C.

Bake in oven for 20 minutes, or until pie is piping hot and cheese is browned.

DESSERT

When we were kids we always had pudding after our dinner. Nowadays, dessert is reserved for special occasions, which means if you are going to bother it should be really worth bothering about. Don't waste the calories on a dessert that isn't fabulous. There is no need to serve big portions of dessert, as often guests appreciate just a small taste of something sweet.

LEMON VERBENA PANNA COTTA WITH PASSIONFRUIT JELLY

Plant a lemon verbena bush just so you can have fragrant leaves to add to desserts like this. It's quite a unique flavour.

→

Lemon Verbena
Panna Cotta with
Passionfruit Jelly

SERVES 8

1 recipe Passionfruit Jelly (below)
16g (2 tblsp) powdered gelatine
500ml (2 cups) milk
500ml (2 cups) cream
100g (½ cup) castor sugar
8 lemon verbena leaves (crushed)

+ Distribute Passionfruit Jelly into bases of non-reactive ramekins or timbales. Leave to set.
+ Mix the gelatine with 125ml (½ cup) milk, stir to combine and leave for a few minutes to soften gelatine.
+ Pour the remaining milk and the cream into a heavy-based saucepan. Add the sugar and lemon verbena leaves and stir over a medium heat until sugar is dissolved.
+ Bring the mixture to the boil and remove from the heat. Leave to sit for at least 30 minutes for the flavour to infuse.
+ Return saucepan to the heat and bring back to just under boiling point. Remove from heat, add softened gelatine and stir until gelatine is dissolved. Cool and when totally cool strain and pour into timbales on top of the jelly.
+ Chill Panna Cotta for at least 4 hours or overnight.
+ To turn the Panna Cotta out, gently pull the edges away from the sides of the dish (this releases the vacuum), shake the dish once or twice and tip the Panna Cotta onto plate.

PASSIONFRUIT JELLY

FOR 8 PANNA COTTA BASES

1 level tsp powdered gelatine
100ml passionfruit juice

+ Soften gelatine in 25ml of the juice.
+ Pour remaining juice into a pot and heat to below boiling. Remove from heat.

MASCARPONE ICE-CREAM WITH SUMMER BERRIES

**Mascarpone
Ice-cream with
Summer Berries**

Limoncello is an Italian lemon liqueur, and is used here not so much as a flavouring but as an acidity regulator to cut down the richness of the recipe. Limoncello is extremely high in alcohol, so measure very judiciously. This recipe makes enough ice-cream to three-quarter fill six 250ml wine glasses, or one 25 x 9 x 7cm loaf tin.

SERVES 6–8

½ vanilla bean (sliced lengthways)
175g mascarpone
2 eggs (separated)
125g icing sugar
50ml Limoncello
250ml cream (lightly whipped)
600g mixed berries (e.g. strawberries,
   raspberries, redcurrants)
icing sugar to garnish

Scrape seeds from vanilla bean and add seeds to mascarpone (reserve pod for use at a later date).

In a large bowl beat together vanilla seeds, mascarpone, egg yolks, icing sugar and Limoncello.

In a separate bowl whisk egg whites until soft peaks form. Gently fold first measure of cream and egg whites into mascarpone mixture (add egg whites in 2 batches to 'loosen' the mixture first).

Pour mixture into mould(s) (if your mould is aluminium, line with plastic wrap first), cover and freeze for at least 4 hours, but preferably overnight.

Approximately 5 minutes before serving, remove ice-cream from freezer and serve with berries. Sieve icing sugar over berries and serve immediately.

ESTHER'S GINGERBREAD

Esther Woollaston, quilt maker extraordinaire, worked out front for Ruth Pretty Catering. It's not just chefs I hit up for recipes! This is the best gingerbread I have ever tasted. Try it for dessert with Kikorangi, the very creamy blue cheese from Kapiti Cheeses, and Jo-Anne Tracey's Sweet Semi-dried Figs (below).

→

Esther's
Gingerbread

with

Jo-Anne Tracey's
Sweet Semi-dried
Figs

MAKES 1 LOAF/CAKE

280g (2 cups) flour
200g (1 cup) brown sugar
1 tsp baking soda
1 tsp baking powder
2 dessertspoons powdered ginger
½ tsp mixed spice
½ tsp ground nutmeg
1 tsp ground cinnamon
360g (1 cup plus ⅓ cup) golden syrup
225g butter (roughly diced)
2 eggs (lightly beaten)
250ml (1 cup) milk

+ Preheat oven to 150°C.
+ Grease and line the base of an 11 x 30cm loaf tin (or alternatively a 23cm square tin).
+ Into a large bowl sift flour, brown sugar, baking soda, baking powder, ginger, mixed spice, nutmeg and cinnamon.
+ In a small saucepan melt golden syrup with butter.
+ To the dry ingredients add the golden syrup mixture, followed by eggs and milk. Combine ingredients well, using a whisk (this is a very wet mix). Pour into prepared tin.
+ Cook in loaf tin for 1 hour 10 minutes (in the square tin for 45 minutes), or until metal cake skewer comes out clean. When cooked, leave in tin to cool for 30 minutes or more before turning out.
+ Serve warm or cold. Esther's Gingerbread also freeze well.

JO-ANNE TRACEY'S SWEET SEMI-DRIED FIGS

These will be the most exquisite dried figs you have ever tasted – slightly chewy, moist and sweet. You will obtain the best result using a dehydrator. Store in the refrigerator for up to one month or in the freezer for up to one year.

400g (2 cups) sugar
1.5 litres (6 cups) water
500g (12) ripe figs

+ Place sugar and water into a heavy-based pot. Stir over a low heat until the sugar dissolves. Increase heat and bring to the boil.
+ Using a cake tester, prick figs all over, piercing the skin. Add figs to the boiling syrup. Cut a double layer of baking paper to fit the pot. Sit the paper directly on top of the syrup to prevent the figs from bobbing above

the surface of the syrup.
+ Reduce heat and simmer the figs for 3 hours, covered with the paper. Remove the figs from the syrup and place on a cake rack to drain for around 30 minutes. (Reserve the syrup for next time you make this recipe.)
+ Place figs in a dehydrator on 55°C and leave to dry for 24–30 hours depending on the size of your figs.
+ Alternatively, place the figs onto a baking tray. Place in a preheated oven at 75°C for 5 hours. Without opening the door, turn oven off, and leave the figs to finish drying overnight.
+ Cool to room temperature and serve.

BAKED ORANGES

←

Baked Oranges

Serve these with a wedge of Saffron Cake (see page 130), or a wedge of Chocolate Mousse Cake (see page 147). Cook them in the oven until the orange skin looks almost glassy.

YIELDS 32 WEDGES, SERVES 8–10

4 (1kg) thin-skinned oranges
water
240g (1 cup plus 4 tblsp) sugar
375ml (1½ cups) water
45ml (3 tblsp) Grand Marnier liqueur

+ Place oranges into a medium-sized pot and cover with water. Bring to the boil, then keep boiling for 20 minutes.
+ Drain oranges and cover with more cold water. Bring to the boil and keep boiling for 5 minutes.
+ Carefully, so as not to break the skin, drain oranges and cool for 15 minutes.
+ Preheat oven to 180°C.
+ Cut each orange (including peel) into 8 wedges, and arrange snugly, with the cut side down, in a non-reactive gratin dish.
+ Make a syrup by combining sugar and the 375ml water in a pot. Stir over a medium heat until sugar is dissolved and then bring to the boil.
+ Pour syrup over oranges and bake in oven for 1 hour or until liquid is syrupy and skin is soft. Turn oranges over halfway through baking. Thicker-skinned oranges will take longer.
+ Pour Grand Marnier over oranges and cool.
+ Chill wedges, covered, for at least 3 hours or overnight. Serve at room temperature.

BUTTERSCOTCH CRÈME BRÛLÉE

A very satisfying butterscotch-flavoured Crème Brûlée. The perfect ending to a meal, served with a glass of sweet rich dessert wine.

→
Butterscotch Crème
Brûlée

SERVES 6

6 egg yolks
45g (¼ cup firmly packed) brown sugar
250ml (1 cup) milk
500ml (2 cups) cream
100g (½ cup) sugar
125ml (½ cup) water
1 tsp salt
5ml (1 tsp) vanilla essence
sugar for brûlée

+ Preheat the oven to 150°C.
+ Using a hand whisk, lightly whisk egg yolks until smooth. Set aside.
+ Heat the brown sugar, milk and cream over a medium-high heat, stirring to dissolve brown sugar. Scald the mixture (do not boil) and remove from heat.
+ While brown sugar/cream mixture is heating, stir sugar and water over low heat in a heavy-based saucepan to dissolve. Increase the heat and, without stirring, bring to the boil.
+ Keep cooking with no stirring until sugar/water turns to caramel (it will be a dark amber colour). Carefully and slowly pour the hot cream into the caramel and stir. (Be careful as it may spit at you.)
+ Gently and slowly hand whisk the mixture into the egg yolks (you do not want to create a froth). Stir in the salt and vanilla essence.
+ Strain to remove any egg particles. Let the mixture sit for 5 minutes and scrape off any froth.
+ Pour custard into soufflé dishes (we use 6 145ml soufflé dishes). Set soufflé dishes in a roasting pan and pour hot water into pan to come halfway up the sides of the dishes.
+ Bake in oven for 35 minutes or until just set. Remove soufflé dishes from roasting pan, cool and then refrigerate for at least three hours, or overnight.
+ When you are ready to serve, sprinkle with sugar, then brown the sugar with a cook's brûlée torch (or place soufflé dishes under a hot grill for a very short time only as you need to keep the custard cold).
+ Serve immediately.

CRÊPES WITH CRÈME DE CASSIS SAUCE

←
**Crêpes with Crème
de Cassis Sauce**

We like to make this dessert in front of guests. Set up a small gas burner on the buffet table.

30g (3 tblsp) butter
150g (1 cup) blackcurrants (fresh
    or frozen)
225g (2 cups) boysenberries (fresh
    or frozen)
60g (6 tblsp) sugar
150g (1⅓ cups) raspberries
    (preferably fresh)
40ml (8 tblsp) crème de cassis
12 crêpes (below)

- In a heavy-based frypan melt butter over a low heat.
- Add blackcurrants and boysenberries to the frypan and sprinkle with sugar. Cook over low heat for 2–3 minutes until juices from berries just begin to run.
- Gently turn the fruit to combine the sugar, and continue until the sugar is dissolved. (You are aiming to keep the berries whole.)
- Add raspberries to the frypan and gently stir to just combine and heat raspberries through.
- Pour in crème de cassis (if you wish create a flambé effect), stir and cook for a further 2–3 minutes or until juices become syrupy.
- Spoon hot Crème de Cassis Sauce onto 1 half of each crêpe and fold over.
- Serve with softly whipped cream or vanilla ice-cream.

CRÊPES

Crêpe batter can be prepared and left overnight if you wish. We make batches of crêpes and freeze them with plastic wrap between each crêpe. For frozen crêpes, before serving allow one hour for thawing and reheat in a crêpe pan as you need them.

150g (1 cup plus 2 tsp) flour
1 egg
2 egg yolks
1 tblsp castor sugar
600ml (2 cups plus ⅓ cup plus
    1 tblsp) milk
50g butter (melted)
oil for greasing crêpe pan

- Sieve flour into a bowl, make a well in the centre of flour and add egg, egg yolks and sugar. Whisk well to combine.
- Gradually add milk and whisk to incorporate all the flour. Rest for 20 minutes (this gives the gluten particles in the flour time to swell and blend well with the milk).
- When ready to use the batter, add butter and whisk well.
- Place crêpe pan on a medium high heat (with no grease at all) for 2–3 minutes or until very hot.
- Pour some oil into the hot pan, it must sizzle, then pour excess back into a small bowl (this greases the pan lightly so that the crêpe does not float in oil and ensures the pretty lace marking which is typical of a real French crêpe).
- Pour a small amount of batter into the pan. Turn the pan so the batter coats the bottom of the pan with a very fine coating. Turn the crêpe over carefully with a palette knife when the edge is lightly browned.
- Cook lightly on the second side, and then remove with a palette knife onto a tray. Cool. Sit crêpes at room temperature until required or freeze.

SPICED FRUIT COMPOTE

If you don't have one or other of the dried fruits, try substituting different dried fruits. Spiced Fruit Compote can be made up to two weeks in advance if stored in a sterilised jar in the refrigerator. A jar of Spiced Fruit Compote makes a more-than-acceptable gift. Muscat wine is a rich sweet dessert wine made from muscat grapes.

→
Spiced Fruit
Compote

SERVES 8

1 cinnamon stick
6 juniper berries
4 cloves
1 vanilla bean (split in half lengthways)
6 coffee beans
125g dried figs (halved vertically)
50g dried pear halves (halved lengthways)
50g dried apricot halves
50g dried peach halves (halved lengthways)
250ml (1 cup) muscat wine
125ml (½ cup) clear apple juice
140g (1 medium) pear (peeled, cored and thickly sliced lengthways)
130g (1 medium) apple (peeled, cored and thickly sliced)

+ In a non-reactive saucepan combine cinnamon, juniper berries, cloves, vanilla bean, coffee beans and dried fruit. Pour muscat and apple juice over mixture, bring to the boil, and simmer for 15 minutes over a low heat.
+ Add fresh pear and apple, cover and gently cook for a further 10 minutes or until fruit is fork tender. Remove from heat, cover and stand for 30 minutes. Transfer to sterilised jars, cover and allow to cool. Store in refrigerator for at least 1 day, but preferably for 3–5 days (the flavour will improve over time).

SAFFRON CAKE

A very good afternoon tea cake with a cup of Earl Grey tea, but also excellent at dessert time with poached or baked fruit and sweetened, lightly whipped cream, flavoured with rosewater.

→
Saffron Cake

MAKES 1 25CM SQUARE CAKE

1 tsp dry breadcrumbs
½ tsp anise seeds (crushed)
40g (4 tblsp) butter (softened)
170g (1 cup) Manuka honey
120g (½ cup) sour cream
4 eggs (yolks and whites separated)
280g (2 cups) pastry flour
½ tsp saffron (ground to a powder in a mortar)
½ tsp baking soda
1 tblsp cream of tartar
2 tsp poppy seeds
edible gold paint (optional)

+ Preheat oven to 175°C. Grease a 25cm cake tin.
+ Combine breadcrumbs and anise seeds and sprinkle evenly over the base of the tin. Set aside.
+ Cream the butter and honey until smooth, add sour cream and beat well.
+ Whisk egg yolks until creamy and combine with honey mixture.
+ In a separate bowl sift together flour, saffron, baking soda and cream of tartar 3 times to ensure even distribution of saffron. Sift this into the batter and fold together gently.
+ Beat egg whites until stiff peaks form, then fold into batter.
+ Pour batter into prepared tin, spreading evenly. Scatter the poppy seeds on top.
+ Bake for 25–30 minutes or until a skewer inserted comes out clean.
+ If you wish, paint patterns on cake with edible gold paint.

SHELLEY'S PARISIAN CHOCOLATE BOMBE

This is my friend and colleague Shelley Templer's version of Jean-George Vongerichten's famous chocolate pudding. Make it ahead, freeze as per the instructions and cook when your guests are ready. Use the best quality chocolate you can afford. We make this dessert with Belgian chocolate or occasionally go for broke with the French brand 'Valrhona'.

SERVES 8

10g (2 tsp) butter (melted)
100g chocolate (roughly chopped)
100g butter (roughly chopped)
2 eggs
2 egg yolks
60g (6 tblsp) castor sugar
50g (7 tblsp) flour

- Brush 6 100ml ovenproof moulds with melted butter.
- In a double boiler over a gentle heat melt chocolate and second measure of butter, stirring occasionally, until melted and glossy. Remove from heat and allow to cool slightly.
- Whisk eggs, egg yolks and sugar until pale and thick.
- Gently fold in sifted flour, then add chocolate mixture and stir to combine (avoid over-mixing as this will make the puddings tough).
- Pour mixture into prepared moulds, cover well with plastic wrap and freeze overnight or for up to 3 weeks.
- When ready to serve, preheat oven to 220°C. Place moulds from freezer onto oven tray and bake for 10–12 minutes or until mixture is firm around the edge. The tops will have risen and will feel dry to the touch, but the centre will be hot and runny.
- Remove tray from oven, carefully run a knife around the edge of mould and turn out onto 6 serving plates. Serve immediately!

←
Shelley's Parisian
Chocolate Bombe

CARAMEL ICE-CREAM

If you do not have a churn, place ice-cream in a deep plastic bowl in the freezer. Every 30–40 minutes bring the bowl out of the freezer and, using an eggbeater, beat to break any ice crystals forming. Continue to do this until ice-cream freezes. The more you beat the ice-cream, the smoother it will be.

→

Caramel
Ice-cream

SERVES 8

500ml (2 cups) milk
500ml (2 cups) cream
8 egg yolks
315g (1½ cups) castor sugar

To make crème anglaise:
+ Combine milk and cream in a medium pot and bring to the boil.
+ Whisk egg yolks until light and fluffy. Gradually add milk to yolks, whisking well to combine. Transfer custard back to the pot and cook over a gentle heat, stirring continuously, until mixture coats the back of a wooden spoon. Set aside.

To make caramel:
+ Combine sugar and 1 tablespoon of water in a heavy-based saucepan. Place over a high heat, swirling the pot occasionally. (Brush sides of pot with a wet pastry brush to help dissolve any sugar crystallising on sides.)

To combine crème anglaise and caramel:
+ Once a deep caramel colour is reached, whisk caramel into crème anglaise until smooth. Strain mixture through a sieve and cool.
+ Churn in ice-cream churn and store, covered, in freezer.

SHERRY ICE-CREAM

There is an exceptionally divine range of sherries called Emilio Lustau. Any of the dessert-style sherries from that range would be perfect for this ice-cream, but we use Pedro Ximenez San Emilio, which is the most dense and concentrated of them all. Serve the ice-cream with Shelley's Parisian Chocolate Bombe (see page 133) and/or Spiced Fruit Compote (see page 130).

SERVES 8

100g (½ cup) castor sugar
125ml (½ cup) water
6 egg yolks
1 tsp orange zest
60ml (¼ cup) Pedro Ximenez
San Emilio sherry
250ml (1 cup) cream
(lightly whipped)

+ In a small saucepan over a low heat dissolve sugar and water by stirring with a metal spoon. Bring to the boil then, without stirring, simmer until small bubbles run across the top of syrup.
+ Place egg yolks into a bowl and whisk until pale and double in volume.
+ Pour syrup in a thin stream into yolks while whisking. Whisk mixture until cold (it will be thick and pale), then add orange zest and sherry.
+ Fold in cream. Place ice-cream into a container, cover and freeze overnight (it will keep for up to a week covered in the freezer).

TWO-TIERED GIN AND TONIC CAKE WITH SUGARED FRUIT

This is a very good birthday cake for grown-ups. You can add candles if you wish.

←
Two-tiered Gin and
Tonic Cake with
Sugared Fruit

SERVES 20

**1 recipe Gin and Tonic Cake
  (see page 138)**
**1 recipe Gin and Tonic Syrup
  (see page 139)**
**1 recipe Lemon Icing
  (see page 139)**
**1 recipe Sugared Fruit
  (see page 139)**

- Cut tops off cakes to make them level, but also to adjust height so that they are even.
- Turn the larger cake upside down onto your selected serving tray. Turn the smaller cake upside down and centre it on top of the large cake.
- Pour the Lemon Icing over the top cake and let it drizzle onto the second cake. Using a metal spatula, spread the icing to form a thin layer over the two cakes.
- Let the icing dry for at least an hour before decorating with the Sugared Fruits.
- Place Sugared Fruits decoratively on the top cake and around the top edge of the bottom cake.

GIN AND TONIC CAKE

MAKES 1 25CM ROUND CAKE AND 1 17CM
ROUND CAKE

415g butter (diced and softened)
660g (3⅛ cups) castor sugar
13 eggs
25ml (1 tblsp plus 2 tsp) gin
25ml (1 tblsp plus 2 tsp) tonic water
zest of 2 lemons and 2 oranges
420g (3 cups) flour
17g (1 tblsp plus 1 tsp) baking powder
1 recipe Gin and Tonic Syrup
   (opposite)
1 recipe Lemon Icing
   (opposite)

- Preheat oven to 180ºC.
- Spray and flour a 25cm and a 17cm round cake tin.
- In a food processor cream butter and sugar.
- Break eggs into a jug and pour them through the feed tube with the processor running.
- Pour the contents of the processor bowl into a large mixing bowl.
- Add gin, tonic, zest, flour and baking powder and stir well to combine. (If you have a large domestic food processor or one with a strong motor, e.g. Cuisinart, the dry ingredients and flavourings could be incorporated in the food processor.)
- Pour mixture evenly into prepared tins and bake large cake for 50–60 minutes and small cake for 40–50 minutes or until a skewer inserted comes out clean.
- Leave cakes to rest for 10 minutes.
- Pour gin and lemon syrup slowly over warm cakes, spreading with a pastry brush to ensure an even coating.
- Leave cakes to cool in tin before removing.

GIN AND TONIC SYRUP

180ml (⅓ cup plus 2 tblsp) gin
50ml (3 tblsp plus 1 tsp) tonic
250g (1¼ cups) sugar
zest of 2 lemons

Place ingredients in a small saucepan. Stir over a low heat until sugar dissolves and then bring to the boil. Boil gently until a syrupy consistency is achieved (this will take about 5 minutes).

LEMON ICING

FOR A 2-TIERED CAKE

380g (2¼ cups) icing sugar (sieved)
1½ tsp lemon zest
70ml (4½ tblsp) lemon juice
20ml (1 tblsp plus 1 tsp) extra light olive
  oil or canola oil

In a small bowl combine all ingredients and whisk until smooth.

SUGARED FRUIT

Fruit can be sugared for up to two days ahead.

TO DECORATE A 2-TIERED CAKE

a selection of fresh small fruits with
  skins (e.g. kumquats, grapes, figs,
  redcurrants, blackcurrants)
a few small kumquat, lemon or orange
  leaves or small grape leaves
1 egg white (lightly whisked)
210g (1 cup) castor sugar

Wash and thoroughly dry all the fruit and leaves.

Using a pastry brush, brush the fruit and leaves with egg white. Shake off any excess.

Thoroughly sprinkle fruit and leaves with the castor sugar to obtain an even coating.

Set fruit aside on a dry tray at room temperature for at least 2 hours, or overnight, before decorating the cake. Do not refrigerate.

SUMMER TRIFLE

A good trifle is the best dessert in the world, and this is an extremely good trifle. It is not nearly as good using a store-bought sponge.

SERVES 10–12

60ml (4 tblsp) medium sherry
250ml (1 cup) peach syrup (reserved from
   Poached Peaches) (see page 143)
1 recipe Multi-versatile Sponge (below)
250g (¾ cup) raspberry jam
400g raspberries
1 recipe Poached Peaches (see page 143)
1 recipe Trifle Custard (below)
330ml (1⅓ cups) cream (whipped)

- Combine sherry and peach syrup.
- Spread the sponge generously with raspberry jam and cut into cubes approximately 3cm square.
- Place sponge cubes into a large glass bowl and sprinkle with raspberries. Pour combined sherry and peach syrup over raspberries. Toss gently to encourage the sponge to soak up the liquid.
- Cut each peach half into 4 even slices.
- Place peach slices over sponge cubes and pour custard over the top. Cover and refrigerate for 3–4 hours.
- Lavishly decorate with cream and serve.

MULTI-VERSATILE SPONGE

A good sponge cake is very useful for many desserts such as wonderful dessert lamingtons, raspberry kisses or butterfly cakes. We often make sponge cake in a bun tray and cut out shapes with a cookie cutter. Your supermarket may stock cake flour – it is a light flour.

MAKES 1 32 X 32CM BUN TRAY

3 eggs
pinch salt
125g (½ cup plus 1 tblsp) sugar
50g flour (preferably cake flour)
25g (8 tsp) cornflour
1 tsp baking powder

- Preheat oven to 190°C.
- Grease and line baking tray (our bun tray measures 32 x 23cm and is similar to a sponge roll tin).
- Begin whisking eggs and salt, slowly pour in sugar and whisk until thick and pale yellow.
- Sift flour, cornflour and baking powder together and fold gently into egg mixture.
- Pour mixture into baking tray.
- Bake for 15–20 minutes or until sponge springs back when lightly touched.
- Leave in tray for 10 minutes before turning out onto a cooling rack.

TRIFLE CUSTARD

MAKES 600ML

6 egg yolks
50g castor sugar
2 tsp cornflour
550ml cream
45ml (3 tblsp) Amaretto liqueur

- Whisk together yolks, sugar and cornflour.
- In a small pot heat cream to just before the boil. Remove from heat and, while stirring, pour a little into the egg mixture. Then gradually add the rest, stirring continuously.
- Return mixture to the pot and stir over a low heat until thick and custardy. Remove from heat and pour into a chilled bowl.
- Add Amaretto, stir and set aside to cool.

RASPBERRY KISSES

Amazingly delicious with home-made fresh raspberry jam. Keep the leftover bits of sponge and freeze so you can make a trifle at a later date.

Raspberry Kisses

SERVES 4

1 recipe Multi-versatile Sponge
  (see page 140)
135g (8 tblsp) raspberry jam
250ml (1 cup) cream (lightly whipped)
100g raspberries
icing sugar to serve

- Using a cookie cutter, cut out 8 7.5cm rounds from sponge.
- Spread a tablespoon of raspberry jam on each round.
- Spoon a good dollop of cream on top of jam on 4 sponge rounds. Top cream with raspberries.
- Place the second sponge round on top of the raspberries.
- Sieve icing sugar over Raspberry Kisses and serve immediately.

POACHED PEACHES

For a not-so-perfect trifle use tinned peaches, but it will never compare to a trifle made with poached peaches. If peaches bob above the surface of the syrup, cut out a greaseproof paper round the diameter of the saucepan and place on top of the liquid.

650g (5–6) peaches
300g (1½ cups) sugar
750ml (3 cups) water

- Cut peaches in half vertically following the natural line of the peach. Using a melon baller, scoop out stones.
- In a wide saucepan combine sugar and water. Over a medium heat stir until sugar is dissolved. Increase heat and without further stirring bring to the boil.
- Add peaches to syrup, cut side up. Bring syrup back to the boil and simmer peaches on one side for 3–5 minutes, Turn peaches cut side down and cook a further 2–3 minutes or until peaches are tender but not soft (cooking time will depend on the ripeness of the peaches).
- Remove peaches from syrup and set aside to cool. Retain peach syrup for use in trifle.

PINOT NOIR AND SUMMER BERRY JELLY

A very refreshing dessert. We often make smaller versions in shooter glasses. This recipe three-quarter fills eight 125ml-sundae glasses.

→

Pinot Noir and
Summer Berry Jelly

SERVES 8

350g (1½ cups) castor sugar
500ml (2 cups) pinot noir
3 star anise

If you are using fresh berries:
14g (4 tsp) gelatine
120g raspberries
120g blueberries
120g blackberries

If you are using frozen berries:
20g (6 tsp) gelatine
180g frozen raspberries
180g frozen blueberries
180g frozen blackberries

+ Place sugar, pinot noir and star anise into a saucepan over a gentle heat. Stir until sugar is dissolved. Increase temperature and heat to just below boiling.
+ Strain syrup, and dissolve gelatine in 125ml (½ cup) of the syrup. Return to remaining syrup and stir. Leave to cool.
+ Put layers of fruit in sundae glasses and then cover with pinot noir syrup.
+ Refrigerate for at least 2 hours or until set.

CHOCOLATE MOUSSE CAKE

In this recipe one simple mixture gives you the cake and the filling. Serve with fresh raspberries and whipped cream.

← Chocolate Mousse Cake

MAKES 10–15 WEDGES

200g dark chocolate (broken into pieces)
125g unsalted butter (cut into pieces)
7 eggs (separated)
210g (1 cup) castor sugar
pinch salt

- Preheat oven to 165°C.
- Spray or grease a round 24cm springform tin and line the base with baking paper.
- Place chocolate and butter into a bowl that fits snugly over a pot of simmering water. Stir until chocolate and butter are just melted. Don't allow this mixture to get hot.
- Whisk egg yolks with 160g (¾ cup) sugar until mixture becomes pale. Keep whisking and slowly pour in chocolate and butter mixture. Whisk until the mixture is thick and creamy.
- In a very clean bowl whisk egg whites with salt and as they become frothy, keep whisking and slowly pour in remaining castor sugar.
- Whisk until soft peaks form.
- Using a big metal spoon fold egg whites into chocolate mixture.
- Pour three-quarters of mixture into prepared tin and place remaining mixture to one side.
- Bake cake for approximately 35 minutes or until cake springs back when you prod it. It should still be moist and slightly wobbly.
- Remove cake from oven and leave in tin on a cooling rack (the middle will drop).
- When cake is completely cold, remove from tin and fill the dropped centre with the uncooked batter.
- Serve immediately or the next day.

**Ruth Pretty's
Christmas Pudding**

recipe page 150

CHRISTMAS

This chapter is for people who truly love to
cook because these people love festivities
and the food associated with them.

RUTH PRETTY'S CHRISTMAS PUDDING

A lighter than usual version of a Christmas pudding. After eating this you are still mobile for the rest of the day! Serve with Brandy cream (opposite).

MAKES A 1KG PUDDING – ENOUGH FOR
8 SERVES

40g (6) chopped dried apricots
180g (1¼ cups) currants
180g (1 cup plus 2 tblsp) raisins
280g (1¾ cups) sultanas
100g (¾ cup) chopped dates
50g (¼ cup) mixed peel (firmly packed)
50g (¼ cup) chopped cherries
    (firmly packed)
1 carrot (100g) (peeled and grated)
1 apple (100g) (peeled and grated)
zest of 1 orange and 1 lemon
60ml brandy
juice of ½ orange and ½ lemon
100g soft unsalted butter (cubed)
100g (½ cup) brown sugar
2 eggs
1 tblsp golden syrup
105g (1½ cups) flour
½ tsp salt
½ tsp ground ginger
1 tsp ground nutmeg
1 tsp mixed spice
100g (1¾ cups) breadcrumbs
    (firmly packed)
25g (2 tblsp) blanched almonds

+ Soak dried fruit, carrot, apple, orange and lemon zest in the brandy and orange and lemon juice overnight.
+ Cream butter and sugar and add eggs, one at a time, just to combine.
+ Add the golden syrup.
+ Sift flour, salt and spices together and beat into creamed mixture.
+ Combine breadcrumbs and almonds with the brandied fruit and fold this into the butter/flour mixture.
+ Butter pudding basin and lid (we use a stainless-steel pudding basin with a fitted lid) and spoon mixture into pudding basin, packing it down.
+ Put the lid on the pudding basin.
+ Preheat oven to 150°C.
+ Put the pudding basin into a roasting tray and pour hot water into roasting tray to come halfway up sides of pudding basin. Bake for 2–2½ hours until a metal skewer inserted comes out clean.
+ When cool wrap in plastic wrap and store at room temperature until Christmas.

BRANDY CREAM

It is best to prepare Brandy Cream just before serving as the brandy tends to sink to the bottom. If this happens, give the sauce a quick whisk.

SERVES 8–10

4 egg yolks
30g (2 tblsp) castor sugar
60ml (¼ cup) brandy
250ml (1 cup) cream

+ In a small bowl whisk the egg yolks and castor sugar until lemon coloured.
+ Lightly whip the cream in a separate bowl, and gently fold the cream and brandy into the egg yolk mixture.

TO REHEAT RUTH PRETTY'S CHRISTMAS PUDDING

Microwave
+ Remove the pudding from the plastic wrap.
+ Put the pudding on a plate and with the microwave on medium, heat for 15 minutes.
+ Test after 10 minutes, as microwaves often differ in power.

Stovetop
+ Fit a colander over a pot of simmering water and place the pudding, still covered in plastic wrap, into the colander.
+ Be careful to ensure that the water does not come up through the colander.
+ Place a lid over the colander and simmer the pudding for 30 minutes.

Oven
+ Unwrap Christmas pudding.
+ Return to pudding bowl, put lid on and reheat in water bath in a 150°C oven for around 1 hour.

A serving suggestion!
+ Wash and dry half an eggshell. Neaten the edges, using small, sharp scissors.
+ Warm ¼ cup of brandy in microwave for 20 seconds, or in a small pot, until it is 'baby bottle' warm.
+ Push the eggshell half into the top of the pudding and, just before you take the pudding to the table, pour the warmed brandy into the eggshell and set alight.

←
**Chocolate
Truffle Tree**

CHOCOLATE TRUFFLE TREE

A very spectacular centrepiece on a Christmas dessert buffet. Buy or hire a croquembouche mould from a cake decorating shop or a professional kitchen shop.

MAKES 1 45CM HIGH CAKE

**600g (6 cups) flaked almonds (roughly chopped)
120g white chocolate
2 x recipe Chocolate Truffles (below)
Goldilocks**

- Preheat oven to 150°C.
- Lay out almonds on a low-sided bun tray and place in oven for 5–10 minutes, or until almonds are pale golden.
- Place white chocolate in a bowl set over a pot of simmering water and gently warm the bowl. When white chocolate begins to melt, remove from heat and stir until smooth.
- Using a dipping swirl, dip truffles one at a time into the melted chocolate and shake to remove excess chocolate (you will have a little chocolate left over to use when assembling tree). Gently roll the truffles in the almonds until entirely coated. Place onto a flat tray and refrigerate until set and ready to assemble tree.

To assemble tree:
Have 1 30cm base diameter croquembouche mould centered on a serving platter or tray of your choice. Place a large drop of chocolate onto 1 edge of a truffle. Place the truffle, chocolate side down, on the tray. Continue this process with all the truffles to make a complete ring around the mould, remembering that truffles are joined bottom to top and they are not adhered to the mould. Repeat the process, making layers up and around the mould. Continue layers above the top of the mould to achieve a pointed finish with one single truffle on top.
- Decorate simply with a Goldilocks.

CHOCOLATE TRUFFLES

Truffles can be frozen freeflow and stored in airtight bags. The better the quality of the chocolate, the more delicious the Chocolate Truffle Tree. Encourage guests to help themselves to the tree.

MAKES 80–90 TRUFFLES

**600g dark chocolate
60ml (4 tblsp) dark rum
30ml (2 tblsp) milk
200g unsalted butter (diced)
6 egg yolks (lightly beaten)**

- Place the chocolate, rum and milk in a bowl that fits tightly into a pot which contains simmering water. Heat until chocolate is three-quarters melted. Add butter and stir until just melted. Remove from heat and add egg yolks and stir until smooth.
- Refrigerate until firm, stirring occasionally to prevent butter rising to the surface.
- Using a teaspoon or melon baller, scoop out enough mixture to form 1.5cm balls. Chill overnight or until required.

CHEESE CHRISTMAS TREES

Perfect to serve with a Christmas drink.

→
Cheese Christmas
Trees

MAKES 70–80 BISCUITS

250g (1⅔ cups plus 1 tblsp) flour
200g (1⅔ cups) tasty cheese (grated)
50g (¾ cup) Parmesan cheese (grated)
125g unsalted butter (finely diced
   and chilled)
½ tsp freshly grated nutmeg
1 egg (lightly beaten)
cayenne pepper

+ Preheat oven to 180°C.
+ Place flour, cheeses, butter and nutmeg into
  the bowl of a food processor and pulse until
  mixture resembles breadcrumbs.
+ Add egg and quickly process until a ball
  of dough is formed.
+ Rest dough in the refrigerator for at least
  30 minutes.
+ Roll dough to 3mm thickness and cut into
  trees with a small Christmas tree cutter.
+ Lightly dust with cayenne pepper and place
  trees onto greased trays.
+ Bake in oven for 10 minutes or until trees
  are light golden.

FESTIVE STUFFED DATES

Perfect to make and pack as gifts. Serve after the main course as a small fingerfood dessert
with coffee.

→
Festive Stuffed
Dates

MAKES 25

50g (⅓ cup plus 1 tblsp) dried
   apricots (finely chopped)
30g (2 tblsp plus 1 tsp) crystallised ginger
   (finely chopped)
50g (⅓ cup) raisins (roughly chopped)
75ml brandy (warmed)
50g pistachio nuts (toasted and chopped)
560g (25) fresh dates
50g chocolate (melted)

+ Combine apricots, ginger and raisins. Pour
  brandy over fruit.
+ Set aside to macerate for at least 20 minutes
  and then add pistachios.
+ Cut dates along one side and remove stone.
+ Fill each date with a teaspoon of stuffing
  mixture.
+ Using a fork, drizzle chocolate in a diagonal
  pattern over the top of the dates. Refrigerate
  until required.
+ Serve at room temperature.

HOT-ROASTED SCALLOPS AND PRAWNS WITH COGNAC

Serve these as an entrée on Christmas Day, especially if you are not planning to present a flaming Christmas pudding.

→

Hot-roasted Scallops and Prawns with Cognac

SERVES 10 AS AN ENTRÉE

30 prawns
30 scallops (washed and cleaned)
1 recipe Seafood Marinade (below)
sesame oil for cooking
Maldon sea salt and freshly ground black pepper
100ml (⅓ cup plus 1 tblsp) cognac
10 lemon halves to garnish

- Peel prawns, leaving the heads and tails intact, (i.e. remove the back shell only). Using a skewer or pointed knife, remove the veins from the prawns.
- Combine prawns and scallops with Seafood Marinade and chill for 1–2 hours (do not leave overnight as this will cause the seafood to break down).
- Drain marinade from prawns and scallops.
- Preheat oven to 220°C. Place a low-sided baking tray in the oven for 1–2 minutes, or until tray is hot and then brush hot tray with sesame oil.
- Remove tray from the oven and place seafood in a single layer on the tray. Season with salt and pepper.
- Bake for 4–6 minutes or until prawns are pink in colour and scallops are cooked through.
- While seafood is cooking heat cognac to lukewarm (be careful not to overheat as this will burn off the alcohol).
- Transfer prawns and scallops to a serving platter (or individual plates) and pour warmed cognac over and ignite in front of guests.
- Garnish with lemon halves.

SEAFOOD MARINADE

MAKES ENOUGH FOR 10 ENTRÉE SERVES

165ml (⅔ cup) vegetable oil
5cm piece root ginger (peeled and finely chopped)
2 cloves garlic (peeled and finely chopped)
¼ cup finely chopped lemongrass
few sprigs coriander (finely chopped)
few sprigs Italian parsley (finely chopped)

- Combine all ingredients in a non-reactive bowl.

PEARS IN VERJUICE WITH YOGHURT AND MINT

A very fresh, tasty, small-portion dish perfect to serve on Christmas Day as an appetiser.

12 ENTRÉE SERVINGS

1 recipe Savoury Pastry Rounds (below)
1 recipe Sun-dried Pears Poached in
   Verjuice (below)
120g Greek yoghurt
12 mint leaves (finely shredded)
12 (90g) slices prosciutto

+ Just prior to service, place a pastry round on each plate.
+ Drain pears, retain poaching liquid and preserved lime rind, and pat pears dry with paper towels.
+ Top each pastry round with 1 heaped teaspoon yoghurt. Sprinkle mint over yoghurt.
+ Roll prosciutto and place a slice on a pastry round on top of yoghurt. Top prosciutto with a pear and a sliver of preserved lime rind.
+ Drizzle some of the remaining pear poaching liquid around the plate and serve immediately.

SUN-DRIED PEARS POACHED IN VERJUICE

This can be made up to two days before the pears are to be served. However, after two days the acidity of the verjuice will cause the pears to break down. To obtain preserved lime, use the Preserved Lemons recipe on page 58 and substitute limes for lemons.

12 ENTRÉE SERVINGS

150g (12) sun-dried pears
rind of 1 preserved lime (thinly julienned)
375ml (1½ cups) verjuice

+ Into a heavy-based frypan combine the pears, preserved lime skin (reserving flesh for another use) and verjuice. Slowly bring to the boil, then simmer gently for 7–8 minutes. Turn pears over and simmer for a further 7–8 minutes.
+ Set aside and leave pears to cool in the poaching liquid.

SAVOURY PASTRY ROUNDS

12 ROUNDS

2 sheets pre-rolled pastry
egg wash (1 egg mixed with 1
   tblsp water)
60g (2 tblsp) sesame seeds
30g (2 tblsp) finely grated
   Parmesan

+ Preheat oven to 200ºC.
+ Using a 7.5cm round cutter, cut 12 circles from the pastry. Retain offcuts for another use.
+ Brush each pastry round with egg wash (being careful not to brush over edges). Sprinkle with the sesame seeds and Parmesan.
+ Cook for 7–8 minutes until golden on top and base. Cool to room temperature and store in an airtight container.

WARM SALAD OF TURKEY AND HAZELNUTS WITH HAZELNUT DRESSING

This can be an almost instant Christmas dinner.

→
Warm Salad of Turkey and Hazelnuts with Hazelnut Dressing

SERVES 8

1–1.2kg turkey tenderloin
Hazelnut Marinade and Dressing (below)
assorted baby-leafed salad (allow 2 handfuls per person)
olive oil for cooking
2 tblsp red onion or shallot (finely chopped)
2 cloves garlic (peeled and chopped)
200g hazelnuts (lightly roasted and roughly skinned)
fresh herbs and edible flowers
freshly ground black pepper

+ Cut turkey tenderloin into slivers, removing the little piece of muscle.
+ Use half of Hazelnut Marinade and Dressing to marinate turkey slivers for at least 2 hours.
+ When ready to serve, arrange salad on individual plates or on a large serving platter.
+ Drain turkey tenderloin and discard marinade.
+ Heat a heavy frypan and smear with olive oil. When the oil starts to sizzle, toss the red onion and garlic in frypan. When the onion garlic is soft but not browned, add turkey in stages to the frypan.
+ If the turkey is cooked before you are ready to serve, cover with aluminium foil and leave to rest.
+ When you are ready to serve, bring the pan up to heat again. Toss hazelnuts in pan and scatter turkey, hazelnuts, chosen herbs and edible flowers over salad.
+ Drizzle warm salad with remaining dressing and season with black pepper if desired.

HAZELNUT MARINADE AND DRESSING

⅔ cup hazelnut oil (walnut oil would do)
2 tblsp balsamic vinegar
⅔ cup freshly squeezed orange or tangelo juice
2 tblsp finely grated orange or tangelo zest

+ Place all ingredients in a small bowl and mix together.

CRANBERRY, CHESTNUT AND ORANGE STUFFED TURKEY

This is a way of maximising the portion yield of a turkey, but the real benefit of this extremely tasty recipe is that you stuff and cook the turkey one or two days before Christmas and serve it cold. Buy a pre-boned turkey or refer to a poultry cookbook for boning-out instructions.

←

Cranberry, Chestnut and Orange Stuffed Turkey

with

Christmas Potato Stacks

recipe page 164

TO SERVE 20

1 4.5kg turkey (boned out)
1 recipe Cranberry, Chestnut and Orange
   Stuffing (see page 164)
olive oil
Apple and Lavender Jelly (see page 165)

Preheat oven to 190°C.

Place turkey between 2 plastic bags and gently hammer the turkey using a meat mallet until it is an even thickness of meat all over.

Mould the stuffing into an oval shape and pile into the centre of the turkey.

Bring both sides of the turkey skin towards the centre and bring the neck skin up to enclose the stuffing.

Using a cotton string, tie the turkey as you would a rolled roast.

Rub turkey all over with olive oil, place turkey into roasting dish and cook for 1–1½ hours until meat juices run clear after being tested with a meat skewer. (Time will vary depending on the thickness of your stuffing.)

Leave to cool and refrigerate overnight.

Using a sharp knife cut into slices and serve with Apple and Lavender Jelly.

CRANBERRY, CHESTNUT AND ORANGE STUFFING

Prior to stuffing the turkey, fry or microwave a little of the mixture to test for seasoning and adjust if necessary. Chestnut meal may be called chestnut crumbs. We buy it frozen. Growers are slowly getting it into the supermarkets.

TO STUFF A 4.5KG BONED TURKEY

150ml (½ cup plus 2 tblsp) port
120g (1 cup) dried cranberries
80g butter
210g (1½) onions (finely chopped)
50g pork fat (minced)
375g chicken mince
240g pork mince
200g (4 rashers) bacon (minced)
2 eggs (lightly beaten)
15g (3 tsp) salt
2 tsp freshly ground black pepper
¼ tsp ground allspice
2 tblsp finely chopped thyme
1 clove garlic (crushed)
200g (1⅓ cups) pistachio kernels (toasted)
250g (2 cups) chestnut meal
zest of 2 oranges

+ Warm port to just before boiling point, add cranberries and leave them to soak for 20–30 minutes.
+ In a heavy-based pan melt butter, add onion and cook until soft but not browned.
+ Add cranberries and port and bring to the boil. Reduce heat and simmer until liquid is reduced by half. Cool mixture.
+ In a large mixing bowl combine pork fat, chicken, pork and bacon mince, eggs, salt, pepper, allspice, thyme, garlic, pistachios, chestnut meal and orange zest.
+ Add onion and cranberry mixture and combine well.
+ Refrigerate until you are ready to stuff turkey.

CHRISTMAS POTATO STACKS

Sensational with the small new potatoes available at Christmas time. These can be prepared a day ahead and baked just when you are ready to serve.

SERVES 4–6

1kg (12–16) small potatoes (with skins on)
15–30ml (1–2 tblsp) extra virgin olive oil
1 tsp Maldon sea salt
freshly ground black pepper
1 tblsp fennel seeds
1 tblsp chopped thyme or rosemary
sprigs of thyme or rosemary

+ Put potatoes into a pot of boiling salted water and simmer until just about cooked but not soft.
+ Preheat oven to 250°C.

+ Drain potatoes well, and arrange on a lightly oiled baking tray.
+ Using a fish slice, squash each potato until flat and about twice its original diameter.
+ Brush tops with extra virgin olive oil and scatter with salt, pepper, fennel seeds and thyme or rosemary.
+ Bake in oven on top shelf for 20 minutes until potatoes are crisp and golden.

To serve:
+ Stack 3 potatoes on top of each other. Sprinkle each stack with salt, drizzle with extra virgin olive oil and skewer with a sprig of thyme or rosemary.

APPLE AND LAVENDER JELLY

The blueberries in this recipe make the jelly a delightful lavender colour. Try this jelly with pork, turkey or duck. Make it now to give away to friends at Christmas. Apple and Lavender Jelly is best made in small amounts. Try three to four cups of juice at a time only.

MAKES 3 300ML JARS

2kg Splendour or Granny Smith apples
2 litres (8 cups) water
2 lavender sprigs
70g (½ cup) blueberries (fresh or frozen)
250ml (1 cup) white vinegar
sugar
2 tsp very finely chopped lavender

- Chop the apples including skins and core.
- Put into a large saucepan with water, lavender sprigs and blueberries.
- Bring to the boil and simmer for 45 minutes or until apples are soft and mushy.
- Add vinegar and simmer a further 5 minutes.
- Pour the apples into a jelly bag (we use a large piece of muslin). Tie the bag and hang it to drain for at least 2 hours (or overnight), collecting the juice in a container.
- Discard the pulp in the jelly bag. Measure the juice into a preserving pan, bring to the boil and skim to remove any foam or froth.
- Measure hot juice, and to every cup of juice add one cup of sugar. Put back on the heat and stir until sugar is dissolved.
- When sugar is dissolved, bring to the boil and then boil until setting point is reached. Test by putting some cold water in a saucer and dropping in ½ tsp jelly. You will see if the jelly has reached setting point. (This may take 20–35 minutes).
- Pour through a sieve to remove any scum.
- Stir in lavender. Pour into small, clean, hot jars and cover.

ROASTED MUSTARD FRUITS

Use whatever dried or preserved fruit you have on hand. We preserve kumquats and crabapples to use at Christmas time. If you don't preserve fruit substitute with tinned apricots, lychees or even guava, using the syrup as we use kumquat and crabapple syrup.

MAKES 4 CUPS

140g (1 cup) dried pear halves
160g (1 cup) pitted prunes
185g (1 cup) dried figs
165g (1 cup) tenderised figs
220g (1 cup) dried apricots
140g (1 cup) dried peach halves
5 preserved spiced kumquats in syrup
250ml (1 cup) spiced Kumquat Syrup
10 preserved crabapples in syrup
250ml (1 cup) crabapple syrup
1 tblsp mustard powder
2 tblsp yellow mustard seeds
½ tsp salt
230g (1 cup) brown sugar
125ml (½ cup) white wine vinegar
125ml (½ cup) dry white wine

- Place dried and preserved fruits in a roasting tray and sprinkle with mustard powder, mustard seeds, salt and sugar.
- Pour vinegar and white wine over fruits in roasting tray.
- Roast in oven for 20–30 minutes until fruits caramelise. Toss the fruits occasionally so that they cook evenly.

GLAZED HAM ON THE BONE

If you are planning to have a ham over Christmas, serve it hot the first time you eat it. Carve your ham like you would a loaf of bread, cutting down to the bone rather than across.

SERVES 50 DEPENDING ON HAM WEIGHT AS
PART OF A BUFFET

1 large cooked ham on the bone
⅔ cup marmalade (you could use honey
　or brown sugar)
⅓ cup Dijon mustard
250ml (1 cup) sherry, orange juice or
　pineapple juice

- Remove the skin from the ham, leaving a layer of fat on the ham.
- With a sharp knife cut the surface of the ham diagonally at 3cm intervals to form diamond shapes, being careful not to cut into the flesh.
- Place the ham in a roasting tray lined with aluminium foil.
- Heat marmalade with Dijon mustard and stir until it is combined, then strain.
- Pour sherry into roasting tray and brush strained marmalade mixture over ham.
- Bake in a 150ºC oven for 1–1½ hours, basting frequently.
- During the last 20 minutes of baking, you may like to garnish the ham with pickled or preserved fruit.
- Serve with Roasted Mustard Fruits (above).

GOLDEN KUMARA, ASPARAGUS AND HAZELNUT SALAD WITH WALNUT VINAIGRETTE

Make this salad with beans when asparagus is not in season.

→

Golden Kumara,
Asparagus and
Hazelnut Salad with
Walnut Vinaigrette

SERVES 6–8 ON A BUFFET

600g golden kumara (peeled)
olive oil
75g (½ cup) hazelnuts
½ recipe Walnut Vinaigrette (below)
350g asparagus spears (pinged and halved)
Maldon sea salt and freshly ground black pepper

- Preheat oven to 190ºC.
- Cut kumara into 3–4cm chunks. Toss in a little olive oil and hot roast for 10–15 minutes or until tender.
- Toss hazelnuts in olive oil and roast for 5–7 minutes or until golden and then toss in vinaigrette.
- Blanch asparagus in a pot of boiling lightly salted water for 2–3 minutes, or until al dente.
- Place kumara and asparagus into serving bowl, add nuts and vinaigrette and season.
- Toss everything together very gently and serve warm.

WALNUT VINAIGRETTE

MAKES 155ML

125ml (½ cup) walnut oil
30ml (2 tblsp) cider vinegar
1 tsp brown sugar
seeds from 1 cardamom pod (crushed, discard pod)
Maldon sea salt and freshly ground black pepper

- Combine oil, vinegar, sugar and cardamom in a small bowl and whisk well.
- Season to taste.

ICEBERG SALAD

←
Iceberg Salad

A fresh, minty and crunchy salad. Serve in your most glamorous bowl and use it to accompany the Cranberry, Chestnut and Orange Stuffed Turkey on page 163.

SERVES 10

1 iceberg lettuce (cut into wedges)
¼ cucumber (peeled, deseeded and
** sliced thinly)**
140g (1 cup) fresh peas
80g (24) snow peas
30 mint leaves (shredded neatly)
Iceberg Salad Vinaigrette (below)

+ Combine lettuce, cucumber, peas and snow peas in a large mixing bowl.
+ Pour vinaigrette over salad, sprinkle with mint and toss gently.

ICEBERG SALAD VINAIGRETTE

YIELDS 105ML

45ml (3 tblsp) white wine vinegar
60ml (4 tblsp) extra virgin olive oil
Maldon sea salt and freshly ground
** black pepper**

+ Combine ingredients in a small jug. Mix and pour over Iceberg Salad just prior to serving.

CHRISTMAS BAKED PEACHES

Christmas Baked Peaches can be prepared a day in advance, left to sit in the refrigerator and cooked the following day. This is the ideal dessert for guests who don't enjoy overly sweet or rich desserts.

→
Christmas Baked
Peaches

SERVES 8

500g (4) ripe peaches
1 recipe Christmas Fruit Mince (below)
1 recipe Macaroon Topping (below)
125ml (½ cup) verjuice

+ Preheat oven to 180°C.
+ Cut peaches in half and scoop out the stone using a melon baller. Fill cavity with a tablespoon of Christmas Fruit Mince. Entirely cover the fruit mince with Macaroon Topping.
+ Place peaches into a non-reactive baking dish. Pour verjuice around peaches. Bake peaches for 13–15 minutes, or until Macaroon Topping is golden in colour and peaches are tender (test peaches by inserting a metal skewer).
+ Serve warm or cold with cooking syrup drizzled around them.

CHRISTMAS FRUIT MINCE

MAKES 355G

50g (⅓ cup) sultanas
50g (⅓ cup) currants
50g (⅓ cup) raisins
20g (3) stoned dates (softened in
    boiling water)
25g (4) dried apricots (chopped)
25g (2 tblsp) brown sugar
70g (½) Granny Smith apple (peeled and
    finely diced)
65g (1) banana (peeled and mashed)
15ml (1 tblsp) brandy

+ In a food processor with a metal blade fitted place dried fruits and pulse to roughly chop. Transfer into a bowl and add brown sugar, apple, banana and brandy. Mix well to combine.

MACAROON TOPPING

2 egg whites
100g (½ cup) sugar
45g (½ cup) coconut

+ Beat egg whites until they are stiff and gently fold in sugar and coconut.

INDEX

THE RUTH PRETTY
COOKING SCHOOL

The cooking school is a very special culinary learning experience. Located at Springfield, amid the green fields of the Kapiti Coast, the school is situated halfway between Wellington and Palmerston North. Ruth – or a guest presenter from New Zealand or overseas – shows participants how to prepare the dishes on that day's menu. Tips and techniques are shared, questions asked and answered, and stories told. Later, participants sit down for lunch – often outside under the grapevine – to try all the delights they have seen prepared. The meal is accompanied by selected wines from the Ruth Pretty Catering cellar. A great day out!

To receive our cooking school programme, email ruth@pretty.co.nz or phone 06 364 3161 with your mailing details. And see more of Ruth's recipes every Saturday in Wellington's *Dominion Post*.